P9-EDC-096

Ellen Weaver

New Brunswick 1974

THE MYSTERY OF SUFFERING AND DEATH

THE
MYSTERY OF

alba house A DIVISION OF THE SOCIETY OF ST. PAUL
STATEN ISLAND, NEW YORK 10314

SUFFERING
AND DEATH

Michael J. Taylor, S.J.
EDITOR

WITH ECCLESIASTICAL PERMISSION

Library of Congress Cataloging in Publication Data

Taylor, Michael J   comp.
    The mystery of suffering and death.

    CONTENTS: Outler, A. C. God's providence
and the world's anguish.—Hick, J.   A world without
suffering.—McKenzie, J. L. The Son of Man must
suffer. [etc.]
Selected bibliography (p.   )
    1. Suffering. 2. Theodicy. 3. Death. I. Title.
BT732.7.T38   231'.8   72-13294
ISBN 0-8189-0263-9

Copyright 1973 by the Society of St. Paul, 2187 Victory
Blvd., Staten Island, New York 10314.

Designed, printed and bound in the U.S.A. by the
Fathers and Brothers of the Society of Saint Paul,
2187 Victory Boulevard, Staten Island, N.Y. 10314 as
part of their communications apostolate.

                    Current Printing (last digit):

                    9 8 7 6 5 4 3 2

ACKNOWLEDGMENTS

Grateful acknowledgment is made to the following authors and publishers for permission to use material under their copyright:

"God's Providence and Man's Anguish" from **Who Trusts in God: Musings on the meaning of Providence** by Albert C. Outler. Copyright © 1968 by Oxford University Press, Inc. Reprinted by permission.

"A Paradise without Suffering" by John Hick. Reprinted from **Evil and the God of Love** (New York: Harper and Row, 1966) pp. 358-63, with permission of the author.

"The Son of Man must Suffer" by John L. McKenzie. Reprinted from **The Way,** Vol. 7, No. 1 (Winter, 1967), pp. 6-17, with permission of the author and the Editors of **The Way** (a review of contemporary Christian spirituality) published quarterly by English Jesuits (114 Mount St., London W 1 Y, 6 A H, England).

"We Rejoice in Our Sufferings" by Joseph Blenkinsopp. Reprinted from **The Way,** Vol. 7, No. 1 (Winter, 1967), pp. 36-44, by kind permission of the Editors of **The Way** (a review of contemporary Christian spirituality) published quarterly by English Jesuits (114 Mount St., London W 1 Y, 6 A H, England).

"Teilhard de Chardin on Suffering and Death" by Christopher F. Mooney, S.J. Reprinted from the **Journal of Religion and Health,** Vol. 4, No. 5 (October, 1965), pp. 429-440, The Academy of Religion and Mental Health, 16 East 34th Street, New York, N. Y., 10016; substantively the same as pp. 106-121, **Teilhard de Chardin and the Mystery of Christ** © (New York, Harper and

Row, 1966) and © (London: William Collins, Sons and Co., Ltd., 1966).

"The Place of the Sick Person in a Christian Anthropology" by François-H. Lepargneur, O.P. Reprinted from **Theology Digest,** Vol. 16, No. 2 (Summer, 1968), pp. 137-141, with permission of the editors of **Theology Digest,** St. Louis, Missouri.

"The Lord of the Absurd" by Raymond J. Nogar, O.P. Reprinted from **The Lord of the Absurd** (New York: Herder and Herder, Inc., 1966), pp. 149-157, with permission of the publisher.

"The Cross of Our Lord Jesus Christ" (herein titled "The Death of Jesus") by Leonard Johnston. Reprinted from **The Way,** Vol. 9, No. 1 (January, 1969), pp. 3-11, by kind permission of the Editors of **The Way** (a review of contemporary Christian spirituality) published quarterly by English Jesuits (114 Mount St., London, W 1 Y, 6 A H, England).

"The Theology of Death" by George J. Dyer. Reprinted from **Chicago Studies,** Vol. 6, No. 3 (Fall, 1967), pp. 275-296, with permission of the publisher.

"Death as Act" by Robert J. Ochs, S.J. Reprinted from **The Death in Every Now,** © (New York: Sheed and Ward, Inc., 1969), pp. 55-77, with permission of the publisher.

"Death" by Ladislaus Boros, S.J. Reprinted with permission of Search Press, Ltd., London, for world rights in excerpts, pp. 90-109, from **Pain and Providence** (Baltimore: Helicon Press, Inc., 1966).

"The Mystery of Death" by Roger Troisfontaines, S.J. Reprinted from **Theology,** Vol. 73, pp. 433-37, 495-502, (SPCK, 1970), with permission of the author and publisher.

"Resurrection as Hope" by Jürgen Moltmann. Reprinted by permission of Charles Scribner's Sons from **Religion, Revolution and the Future** by Jürgen Moltmann. Copyright © 1969 by Jürgen Moltmann.

"Death and Cosmic Resurrection" by Kilian McDonnell, O.S.B. Reprinted from **The Priest,** Vol. 25, No. 10 (November, 1969), pp. 593-98, with permission of the author and publisher.

"Heaven: The Essence of our Future" by Ladislaus Boros, S.J. Reprinted from **We Are Future** (New York: Herder and Herder, Inc., 1970), pp. 173-75, with permission of the publisher.

CONTENTS

viii   *The Mystery of Suffering and Death*

INTRODUCTION

To keep faith in a time of "future shock" is not easy. The pressures of a rapidly changing, impersonal, permissivist society create whole new sets of problems for the believer. And yet the modern Christian, like his less sophisticated, more relaxed ancestor, readily admits that one of the more distracting problems he faces is not new; it has been around since sentient life began on earth—the mystery of suffering and death.

To attempt to penetrate the mystery is really to decide whether human life is worth the struggle. To many, the question of God's existence depends on how you answer the problem. And if you admit his existence, you begin to have other problems—is God omnipotent, loving and merciful, or is he calculating, vindictive, or maybe just indifferent? Suffering and death are indeed enigmas for man. Why is there so much oppression of the innocent? Why must the good suffer as much as the bad? Why must those for whom we pray, still endure sickness and torment? How can God observe the cruelty and injustice in the world and do so little about it?

And so the questions multiply. Who wishes on us a world of suffering and death? Why is man, supposedly God's image,

weighed down with infirmity and misery? What is the point of
so much bitterness and tragedy? Born with a taste for immortality,
why are we burdened with all this mortality? Why must we suffer
death before a chance at eternal life can be ours? Why must
everything be torn away from us at the end—our life, our friends,
all we have strenuously built up and maintained? Can such a
life claim sensible meaning? Is there a hopeful conclusion to it all?

The Christian is certainly not unbothered by these questions,
but he believes that God has penetrated the mystery of suffering
and death by sending Jesus as a light to pierce its "darkness."
The Christian accepts Christ as the "first and last—the living
one—the man who brings meaning to life and death." From
Apostolic times Christians have been told and have believed
that suffering and death are not without purpose. Christians make
sense of life not by closing their eyes to man's anguish, or by
wishing it away, but by accepting it and opening the darkness of
life to Christ's light.

Our suffering world may seem all too provisional and yet
through Christ we know a victory is in store for it. A definitive,
final victory is even now effective in our lives—*"nothing* can
separate us from Christ's love for us." In a world called to share
God's life there can be no final hopelessness or despair. Even
a suffering world, a world that knows death daily, can have
meaning.

Such a world, to be sure, is not easy to understand or to live
in and the man of faith, no less than the non-believer, needs
meaning to support him in the dark moments of life. He can be
thankful that Christian theologians are re-thinking the problem
of suffering and death, investigating critically how the God of
Creation and his Christ feature in its "solution." Believing scholars
are gaining new insights from anthropology, modern philosophy,
psychology, and a revitalized theology and are giving more positive
expression to the problem, providing more satisfying answers this
time around.

In particular the theology of death is undergoing a remarkable change. Death is no longer seen as a forbidding, fearful
episode in man's life, but, as some say, the time of "deepest self-

fulfillment"—"the opportunity for man's first completely personal act"—"the time of final option," etc. To give the reader examples of the writing of major theologians who are discussing the subject with seriousness and depth, we present this volume of essays. The authors generally are not embarrassed by the traditional treatment of the question. They recognize, however, the inadequacies of earlier interpretations and have re-examined the problem with thoroughness, incorporating into their reflections creative insights from modern science and from contemporary philosophy and psychology. It is hoped that their comments and conclusions will shed further light on a problem for this or any age—the mystery of suffering and death.

MICHAEL J. TAYLOR, S.J.

PART I

THE MYSTERY OF SUFFERING

Chapter One

GOD'S PROVIDENCE AND THE WORLD'S ANGUISH

ALBERT C. OUTLER

There is, of course, no blinking the fact that even a mildly cheerful view of God's providence falls afoul of human anguish—suffering, tragedy, sin, and the fear of death. Here is the stone of stumbling for all those blithe spirits who can, upon occasion, keep singing past the first stanza of "This Is My Father's World."

Existence *is* untoward—it is "thrown," "broken," and experienced as an agony. Any thoughtful man might well imagine that he could have devised a cosmic operation less replete with frustration, suffering, and indignity. And this, for Christians, has been a perennial torment, for the fact of evil brings God's good name into doubt. It is a hazard to belief, a temptation to disbelief. How can it be true that God's sovereign love is "present" in the carnage and wastage of *this* world?

Interestingly enough, this question got its classic form—*whence* evil? (*unde est malum?*)—from the pagan theologians and philosophers, whose answers reflect their several theologies. In the teachings of the popular religions, evil was regarded as a by-product: of the careless antics of the sky-gods or the purposeful cruelties of the earth-gods. In either case, the gods, preoccupied with their own affairs, were not themselves affected by the mischief or misery they wreaked. The religious philosophers from Socrates to Plotinus rightly regarded such notions as profoundly immoral— and said so. This is why Socrates was executed as an atheist and why, in return, Plato barred "the poets" (spokesmen for the popular mythologies) from his ideal community. For the Platonists, evil was identified as the privation or corruption of the good (itself identified with being). For the Stoics, it was the harvest of unreason and the lack of self-control. For the Epicureans, it was the blind way of the world from which the wise man withdraws as far as possible. In each case, the common effect of these "theodicies" was to disengage the divine from the hurlyburly of ordinary life and to propose a program of aloofness as the right answer to the problem: the mystic way of the Platonists, the way for the Stoics, the way of serene indifference of the Epicureans.

The case stood quite differently with the Christians, who were stuck with their faith in God's sovereign providence in the whole creation, "warts and all." The Old Testament is full of tales of God's complicity in discreditable affairs, and yet it never disavows his final responsibility for the world and its ways. Indeed, this was the scandal that drove the very first "radical theologian" in the Christian ranks (Marcion) to his desperate efforts to rescue the true Gospel of Love (which he found in his own expurgated canon of the Pauline letters) from its fatal corruption in what by his time had become "traditional Christianity." The Gnostics were able to shake the Christian community to its foundations with their claim that their doctrines cleared the High God's name from any association with the creator of this earthly shambles. This challenge forced the Church into one of its profoundest crises. On the one hand, God had to be cleared of the charge that he was the author of evil and sin, or else the Gospel of his sovereign goodness went down the cosmic drain. On the other hand, if dualism was the only recourse for preserving his goodness, then his provident involvement in creation would have to be abandoned. Orthodoxy staked its integrity on the conjunction of God's sovereignty *and* his goodness and thereby

posed the question that has continued as perennial: how to maintain *both* in the face of man's universal experience of evil.

As usual, the Christians tried everything they could think of—
in one or another of two main tendencies. In their liturgies and
devotions the stress was on God's involvement—the Divine Sacrifice for which the Cross and Eucharist were the effective symbols.
In their metaphysical reflections, however, the accent moved over
to a stress on God's remotion from the finite. Men like Tertullian
and Origen and, thereafter, the Cappadocians and Augustine,
made much of God's transcendence, his invulnerability to change,
passion, degradation—which is to say immutability, im-passibility,
a-seity, etc., etc. (the "attributes" of deity so long familiar to the
philosophers). What held these two divergent tendencies in fruitful
tension was the Christian consensus on God's *com*passion. Moreover, the Christians were blocked off from either of the extremes
of immanence or transcendence because of their prior commitment to the distinctive focus of their faith: the Incarnation of
God's saving love and wisdom in Jesus of Nazareth.

Here again the ways divided. In Irenaeus and the Eastern
theologians, there emerged a type of theodicy which began by
accepting the reality of evil and of God's responsibility for its
existence, together with a matching affirmation of the final triumph
of grace over the interim powers of sin and death. In an excellent
recent book, Professor John Hick has reviewed this Irenaean tradition carefully and uses it as the basis for a persuasive theodicy
for moderns.

Irenaeus sees our world of mingled good and evil as a divinely
appointed environment for man's development towards the perfection that represents the fulfillment of God's good purpose for
him.[1]

The other, and far more massive, tradition in theodicy was
fashioned in and for Latin Christianity by Augustine, and it ran

---

1. John Hick, **Evil and the God of Love,** London: Macmillan, 1966,
   p. 221. The whole section on "The Irenaean Type of Theodicy,"
   p. 207 ff. is worth very careful study.

to the effect that while evil was existentially real enough—nobody ever denied *that!*—it had no essence of its own, no ontic ground. There is a definitive summary of this position in the *Enchiridion* (IV, 12, 13) which is as brief, and far clearer, than a paraphrase would be:

All of nature, therefore, is good, since the Creator of all nature is supremely good. But nature is not supremely and immutably good as is the Creator of it. Thus the good in created things can be diminished and augmented. For good to be diminished is evil; still however much it is diminished, something must remain of its original nature as long as it exists at all. For no matter what kind or however insignificant a thing may be, the good which is its "nature" cannot be destroyed without the thing itself being destroyed. There is good reason, therefore, to praise an uncorrupted thing, and if it were indeed an incorruptible thing which could not be destroyed, it would doubtless be all the more worthy of praise. When, however, a thing is corrupted, its corruption is an evil because it is, by just so much, a privation of the good. Where there is no privation of the good, there is no evil. Where there is evil, there is a corresponding diminution of the good. As long, then, as a thing is being corrupted, there is good in it of which it is being deprived; and in this process, if something of its being remains that cannot be further corrupted, this will then be an incorruptible entity [**natura incorruptibilis**], and to this great good it will have come through the process of corruption. But even if the corruption is not arrested, it still does not cease having some good of which it cannot be further deprived. If, however, the corruption comes to be total and entire, there is no good left either, because it is no longer an entity at all. Wherefore, corruption cannot consume the good without also consuming the thing itself. Every actual entity [**natura**] is therefore good; a greater good if it cannot be corrupted, a lesser good if it can be. Yet only the foolish and unknowing can deny that it is still good when wholly corrupted. Whenever a thing is consumed by corruption, not even the corruption remains, for it is nothing in itself, having no subsistent being in which to exist.

From this it follows that there is nothing to be called evil if there is nothing good. A good that wholly lacks an evil aspect is entirely good. Where there is some evil in a thing, its good is defective or defectible. Thus there can be no evil where there is no good. This leads us to a surprising conclusion: that, since every being, in so far as it is a being, is good, if we then say that a defective thing is bad, it would seem to mean that we are saying that what is evil is good, that only what is good is ever evil and that there is no evil apart from something good. This is because every actual entity is good [**omnis natura bonum est**]. Nothing evil exists in itself, but only as an evil aspect of some entity. Therefore, there can be nothing evil except something good. Absurd as this sounds, nevertheless the logical connections of the argument compel us to it as inevitable.[2]

This is a better argument, I think, than Professor Hick has found it to be.[3] It "explains" how God's grace can remain sovereign and undefeated even while it is being resisted and tainted. It shatters the force of the Manichaean dualism that had bemused Augustine himself and that remains a temptation to those who find it easy to take evil "at face value." It was consistent with the Gospel's promised remedy for the ravages of sin and it reinforced the Christian hope that, in the end, God would be "all in all" (I Cor. 15:28). It stresses, as the Irenaean tradition does not, the metaphysical chasm between being and non-being, between truth and error, between good as positive and evil as privative.

The general line of this Augustinian theodicy was followed in the West—and in the East from John of Damascus—down through Aquinas and Calvin to Karl Barth and Austin Farrer, whose *Love Almighty and Ills Unlimited* is the best of its recent restatements—an "opposite number" to Professor Hick's book.

But it has two liabilities and they are serious. In the first place, it readily appears to a victim of evil as if it were explaining his ills away. Any actual experience of suffering, pain, or indignity is more likely to give rise to consternation, outrage or despair than to the serene realization that it is privative and ultimately unreal. So what if evil is only the corruption of the good? Are we less agonized by its horrid harvest of misery? Evil is felt as a positive *assault* against the good and it adds insult to injury to be told that the stimulus or our anguish is not really real. This privative notion has the merit of denying its antithesis— that God is absent from, or helpless in, these episodes of rampant evil. But its converse implicate—that God's providence is active in even the very worse that happens—is not easily remembered or

2. **Augustine: Confessions and Enchiridion,** Library of Christian Classics, Philadelphia: The Westminster Press, 1955, vol. VII, pp. 343-44.
3. **Op. cit.,** pp. 59-64.

believed when men are being shattered by natural disasters or degraded by sin and inhumanity.

In the second place, this Augustinian perspective complicates the doctrine of providence, to which it is vitally related. In defense of the sovereignty of grace—and this is its chief concern—it inserts the Plotinian notions of immutability and impassibility as necessary ingredients in such a sovereignty. In this view, the notion that God should "suffer" change or passion becomes unthinkable—equivalent to a denial of his power and glory. In liberal Protestantism, on the other hand, there has long been an awareness that the premises of the Augustinian theodicy—Original Sin and the Fall, divine transcendence and the "unreality" of evil—are deeply dissonant in the modern mind. In response, liberalism took the opposite task of relocating surd evil within God's own being—producing a mildly startling distinction between God's good intentions and his ability to perform. Professor E. S. Brightman was probably the most thoughtful exponent of this position,[4] which turned on a sharp disjunction: either divine sovereignty or the divine goodness. Between these two, his choice was clear, and so perhaps it would be for most of us, if it comes to *that* choice.

Further toward the fringe of liberalism there was a variety of efforts to salvage God's goodness—or at least to firm up the ground under human values—by shifting the chief agency for good and evil over onto the human side. Here the hope was raised that natural evil can be largely mastered by science and technology, and no great alarm over the fact that the same technology that conquers natural hazards keeps on generating new threats to human well-being. There was, when I was young, considerable encouragement in the brave thought that not even God could make a Stradivarius without Antonio, but that was before its converse could have been conceived, that not even God could have made an Auschwitz without a Hitler. And I still recall my vivid sense of topsy-turvy when I came upon a poem, on a student assembly bulletin board back in the 'thirties, that told of the con-

---

4. Edgar Sheffield Brightman, **The Problem of God,** New York: Abingdon Press, 1930.

version of an erst-while disbeliever. He had supposed that neither he nor God had any real need of each other, but the sight of Christ on his Cross had brought home the truth that God's cause in this world is in moral danger and desperately needs men to save it. The unforgettable punch line:

Courage, God, I come!

I am very much aware that these comments on the gropings of Christians and others for answers to the inescapable perplexities of good and evil—for there is "the problem of the *good*" as well as evil!—do not amount to a complete or even coherent survey of the enterprise. Nor is there time and space here for a fully developed theodicy, even if I had one to offer.[4a] For my purposes here, a sort of homily must suffice—a sermon that begins with an amateur's reading of the problem in Scripture and that concludes with what I hope is an honest and relevant "application" of the biblical wisdom about "overcoming evil with good" as Christians have tested this in the course of life and in the face of death.

For it strikes me forcibly that the biblical people come at this whole issue of God's presence in the world's torments in a different temper than one sees in the standard theodicies, especially those in the Augustinian succession. Scripture has no misgivings anywhere about God's freedom and omnicompetence. Everywhere, his aboriginality, his divine initiative and resourcefulness and sole deity stand secure against an encompassing polytheism and the chronic defections of his wayward Covenant People. Nobody in the Bible supposes that God's own fate is locked into the fortunes of his creation and it is unthinkable that anything creaturely can finally defeat his purposes. His final goal—the rule of righteousness and the reign of love—is never hedged or sold short. What is more, the theme of God's self-possession is as clear in the "mythological" passages as elsewhere—which is decidedly not the case in the Greek and Oriental mythologies.

4a Happily, however, I can in good conscience urge both Farrer and Hick upon the reader—and Hick if he insists upon a single choice.

It is, therefore, all the more remarkable that what these biblical people are really interested in is God's hazardous involvement in history—tragic and heart-rending as this has been made by man's defiance and his self-stultifying attempts to repudiate God's sovereignty and grace. Genesis gives the classic statement of the theme. God begins the creation as a deliberate venture in developing a community of finitely free creatures capable of blessedness and of sharing in his infinite love. There is an astute commentary on the risks of this venture in one of Thomas Mann's most brilliant chapters ("Prelude in Egypt") where he reports the angelic dissatisfactions with God's enthusiasm for creating *men* when he could have "let matters rest once and for all at [*their*] decent and honorable existence."

> Out of sheer restlessness and lack of exercise; out of the purest "much wants more"; out of a capricious craving to see, after the angel and the brute, what a combination of the two would be like; out of all these motives, and impelled by them [God] entangled himself in folly and created a being notoriously unstable and embarrassing. And then, precisely, he set his heart upon it in magnificent self-will and made such a point of the thing that all heaven was offended.
> . . . With this being, then—in other words, man—evil came into the world. . . . Through the creation of the finite life-and-death world of form no least violence was done to the dignity, spirituality, majesty or absoluteness of a God who existed before and beyond the world. And thus up to now one could not speak seriously of error in any full or actual sense of the word. It was different with the ideas, plans and desires which were now supposed to be up in the air, the subject of confidential conversations with Shemmael [viz., the covenant with a Chosen People, etc.][5]

It was, then, God's free choice to produce an enterprise one part of which would be under the reflex control of divine *fiat* (natural order) and the other (angels and men) with a narrow range of real freedom. In retrospect, it looks like an experiment in which the odds were stacked against success. Adam's chances for preserving his innocence and bliss seem now pathetic. But

---

5. Thomas Mann, **Joseph the Provider,** New York: Alfred A. Knopf, 1944, pp. 4-5, 9.

what was the alternative? Some sort of moral automaton? And would that have been really better, in the long run?[6] We cannot know, of course. What we do know is that the Eden story tells of a God who is undeniably "in charge" but who is also bilked and baulked by his own custom-crafted creatures—and this on either the Irenaean surmise that the first man was created immature so that he could grow up (to "learn by doing"), or on the Augustinian hypothesis of an originally perfect creature who came a fearful cropper over that forbidden fruit

. . . whose mortal taste
Brought death into the world, and all its woes.

This shaky start is then followed, throughout the rest of the Old Testament, by a series of misadventures in which the Almighty is forever having to improvise in response to some new human waywardness and to fall back on Plans B or C. The history of Israel is a very strange story, by any mythological or metaphysical canon you choose: God and man in protracted moral struggle, with no doubt about God's freedom and grace, and yet with almost nothing coming off according to the program. The Chosen People promptly misunderstood their unique role in human history—and the "unchosen" peoples were visibly unimpressed by God's provision for their salvation through Israel. This becomes the burden of the prophets and apocalyptists: God's warfare against unrighteousness and inhumanity; his promise and provision for his knowledge and love "to cover the earth as the waters cover the sea" (cf. Hab. 2:14). Job can raise the doubt, in reverent anguish, that God is just; he can, in high religious con-

---

6. Cf. Hick, **op. cit.,** pp. 301-11, for an interesting "demonstration" that it is logically inconceivable that God could "have so constituted men that they could be guaranteed freely to respond to Himself in authentic faith and love and worship"—because that would have involved the abridgment of human freedom. Hick's analogy for this, following Antony Flew, is the unfree relationship of a hypnotized person to his hypnotist.

science, reject the pious bromides of his false comforters—and
he can be silenced by a show of force that scarcely amounts to
persuasion.

The same pattern continues when we shift to the New Testament. The mission of the Messiah-come-in-the-flesh has one
announced aim ("the lost sheep of the house of Israel" [Matt.
10:6; 15:24]) and yet another actual outcome ("Lo, we turn
to the Gentiles" [Acts 13:46]). The history of the Christian
church begins with illusory hopes of an imminent *Parousia*. And
then, after that first miscalculation, it has continued for nearly
two millennia with perennial crises and transvaluations of its
original mission and message.

These biblical stories are a mirror held up to the human condition. But, whereas in pagan mythology and philosophy, this
picture of God in the Bible would imply a degradation of his
being and glory, in the biblical mind these signs of man's partially
successful resistance to God's designs serve to illuminate the axis-
theme of biblical theology: God's freedom *and* his forbearance,
his unmerited mercy *and* his omnicompetence (as contrasted with
omnipotence). In this view, God's unswerving pursuit of his
goals for man in the midst of the turmoils of human history is an
even more striking proof of his providence and total investment than
any form of aloofness could ever be. For there is never any question as to who has the initiative in nature and history or where
the final power lies. The possibilities of history and the provisions
for the mystery of salvation are what they are by the elect counsel
and design of the Most High, beside whom there is no other.
God reveals his moral expectations (Torah) to men, he pronounces
judgment on their deviations, he visits his wrath on the rebels—
and all this is talked about in language that is frankly anthropomorphic because it is also apophatic. But the purpose of it all
is not the juridical imposition of Torah nor the condign punishment of offenders but rather the gathering of faithful persons into
a fully human community by the various means of moral suasion
of which grace is the chief!

In biblical terms, God's maintenance of his freedom does not
require ontic barriers for his self-defense. Because he really is

sovereign, he truly is free to allow evil as the dark shadow of corrupted good and yet sovereign to veto its final triumph. The sovereignty that reigns unchallenged is not as absolute as the sovereignty that accepts the risks of involvement and yet also provides appropriate resources for human fulfillment even in the depths of tragedy. If this sort of reflection strikes you as a diminution of God's Almighty Power, that, too, is a sign of our ironic situation: i.e. that Christian theodicy has come to rely almost exclusively on notions of immutability and impassibility which were, originally, only hermeneutic aids for interpreting the biblical testimony about a desperately involved God in terms quite different from any of the then reigning polytheisms.

But surely it should be decisive that this biblical witness is summed up in the life and teaching of Jesus Christ—and in his death, resurrection, and triumph. There the problem of evil and God's goodness stands forth in its starkest form—and is answered in a way designed to provide the Christian with his liveliest hope in life and death. The Incarnation is the recapitulation, in a single human life in a specific historical episode, of the entire enterprise of God's judgment, mercy, and sovereign grace in all lives, all times, all circumstances. It is, as you know, a formal and substantial heresy (maintained, however, by many who suppose themselves "orthodox") to interpret Christ's passion and death as a merely human event that left the God-Father unaffected. The Christian tradition understands the Cross in far more scandalous terms:

> O Love divine! what has Thou done?
> The immortal God hath died for me!
> The Father's co-eternal Son
> Bore all my sins upon the tree;
> The immortal God for me hath died!
> My Lord, my Love is crucified.

Here is a traditional version of the "death of God" (dated 1742)— as orthodox as the Definition of Chalcedon.

There is, therefore, no warrant in the Gospel stories for a picture of God as immune from the assaults on love and dignity that are staples of ordinary life. Freely and for love of us all the God-Father sent his only Son into the world—into our history and its tragedies—to expose himself to every stage and sort of human weakness and privation. The point stressed most in the birth-narratives is not the glory of the miracles but the indignity and squalor of the historical circumstances. Moreover, the rest of the Gospels' account is shaped around Christ's sufferance of the powers of evil—out of all due proportion for proper "biographies." Their motive for this is the fact that here is their prime test-case for the whole idea of God's provident presence in the deepest slough of man's despond.

God sends his Messiah to the lost sheep of the house of Israel and they reject his claims—but only as prototypes of all others who will ever thereafter reject them. As an unauthorized rabbi, Jesus distills the quintessence of the Law and the Prophets, only to have it go unheeded by those whose highest concern was the very same righteousness of that Law he was transvaluing for them and for all mankind. His frustration at being ignored by those he sought to serve drove him to tears on the Mount of Olives, to outrage in the Temple. The stories of "Passion Week" are focused on his desolation at the end: Gethsemane, Pilate's tribune, the Via Dolorosa, Golgotha. The nadir of it all is the cry of dereliction matched with a final word of utter trust: "Father, into your hands I commit my spirit."

One need not risk the heresy of patripassianism in order to take all this with profound seriousness. Sabellius' error lay in his confusions of the distinctive "offices and ministries" of the "persons" of the Trinity. But the live nerve of the truth he exposed—and mis-stated—runs through every valid Christology (and theodicy, since the two are finally the same). There *is* a cross in the heart of God. The Provident Mystery is involved in the agony of sin *with us*. It matters more for the triumph of righteousness that grace be finally invincible than that it should ever be irresistible.

Nor does his theme of strength made perfect in weakness end with the resurrection. Pentecost was a brave beginning for the Church but her first centuries are a curious compound of pathos and glory. The first Christians were an insignificant minority, even in Judaism, with sadly mistaken hopes for their future here on earth. The second generation was expelled from the original Jewish matrix and yet also rejected by the Gentiles, accused by the Romans of misanthropy and atheism. The subsequent history of the Church poses the same question in each of the successive crises that she has weathered: how on earth has she survived? No adequate answer seems possible without some reference to some notion of providence.

It is, therefore, an urgent question for contemporary theology as to whether we can replace the traditional theodicies based on God's transcendence with some version of the "theology of the cross" (*theologia crucis*) that yokes Christ's cross with ours. In defense of the divine sovereignty, traditional theology opted for a view of God that lifted him above the malignancies of sin and evil. But this carried one of two implications: either he was above the battle or, if he but passed the word, the world's woes and weeping would vanish. When it was complained that this was not the highest goodness men could conceive (and therefore unworthy of God), the answer was given that God's counsels are inscrutable and his ways past finding out. This brazen begging of the question served to quiet the doubts of some of the faithful but it left the rest with John Stuart Mill's blunt disjunction: if God is able to prevent evil and does not, he is not good; if he would prevent evil and cannot, he is not almighty. Many a sensitive Christian has writhed on the horns of this dilemma, since neither alternative is compatible with the essence of his faith.

Meanwhile, the new paganism, from Voltaire to Sartre, has found the courage or despair to reject the whole scheme *in toto*. Theodicy, in any of its classical forms (Greek or Christian), turns on the prior assumption that being and goodness are correlative, that the matrix of existence is orderly and that evil is, literally, the *ab-surdum*. But there is simply no problem if the matrix itself is absurd and if the only order, freedom, and values are those supplied by human episodes of rational freedom in a context of encompassing unreason. For Heidegger, the untowardness of existence (to which, as a Nazi, he contributed) proves the absence of God. Sartre turned up nauseated from squinting at the surds of existence until he could integrate them in a total ontology of absurdity. What should be noted is that the moral effect of this new paganism is the same as that of the immutability-impassibility doctrines. In both, man is left alone with both his grandeurs and his miseries.

The impassibility doctrines come in two styles: with and without pity. The upholders of sheer sovereign power are led by their pitiless logic to one or another hypothesis about the predetermined damnation of the vast mass of mankind—in whose eternal perdition God's glory shines forth untarnished. For those more tender-hearted, there are the universalist alternatives, which work from the same premise of divine transcendence but with a contrary projection of "last things." Neither of these options is satisfactory for they both decline the risks of "God with us" here in the heart of darkness.

There is yet another complication in the problem of evil in our time. It comes from a steadily decreasing tolerance of human misery by modern men whose hopes have been raised to the level of real confidence that misery can be reduced or banished. Parlous as it is, the human lot today, speaking generally and comparatively, is ampler and more open to improvement than in any age since Eden. And yet far more of us are far more discontented with *our* lot than any generation ever was. Our progress in overcoming the tyrannies of nature—easing pain, enhancing health, postponing death, multiplying creature comforts—has formed a new mind-set that has no precedent in human history: misery is less to be endured than overcome, and man has the means within his grasp to overcome it. What once men suffered mutely as inevitable they now demand relief from because they are convinced it is possible. Markham's "man with the hoe" has become McLuhan's man with TV hypnosis.

But the millennium still awaits and men are still denied the full harvest of the secular apocalypse as advertised. Hunger is still a torment in the world where, we are told, there are ample technical resources to wipe it out. Poverty persists in sight of affluence, the human community disintegrates despite instant (and constant!) communication. Freedom has brought us headaches along with hallelujahs.

And this has generated an imperious mood of aggrieved innocence in modern man—a rising impatience amongst those whose reach has exceeded their grasp (which must surely be most of us). The old pagans blamed their misfortunes on the gods. Our Christian forefathers tended to blame their indignities on nature—and themselves (original sin). It would not now occur to many of us to accuse nature; still fewer are inclined to blame ourselves. "Guilt" is recessive: parents are to blame for their children's alienations, "society" is the scapegoat for the parents, and so it goes. We used to speak of "anxiety *and* guilt"; there was an Age of Anxiety of which W. H. Auden was celebrant. Now the conventional sense of guilt is gone, or going, and in its place resentment runs unchecked. The Age of Anxiety has turned into the Age of Outrage with Dylan Thomas for a bard.

Do not go gentle into that goodnight;
Rage, rage against the dying of the light.

The bitter fruit of all this is a temper of self-righteousness and mutual recrimination that leaves the problem of moral evil and human tragedy less intelligible than ever, and that makes its practical solution quite impossible. If others are to blame for our condition, or for the human condition, then let them rectify it. The part of the offender is to demand that rectification. This temper of injured innocence has gone far to poison intergroup and international relations everywhere.

It may, therefore, be unfashionable but urgent to reconsider the intentions of two traditional doctrines that once shaped the Christian perception of mankind's corporate responsibility for his human woes: original sin and total depravity. Allowing for, and rejecting, the misanthropic excesses to which these notions are susceptible, let us notice their two interdependent aims and functions. They were designed, in the first place, to undercut all claims of human self-righteousness and merit—and so to establish our radical need of God's sheer unmerited favor as the single source of any possible salvation. There are, it may be, other ways to do this. The essential point, however, is that without some such sense of need and dependence, the biblical meaning of faith and reconciliation is stultified. In the second place, the traditional doctrine of "fallen human nature" provided an etiology of moral evil; it "explained" man's misery in terms of his enmity to God and his correlative inhumanity to his neighbor—and himself. Thus, one might think, it would go with our modern accent on man's responsibility for human culture to hold him equally responsible for the spoliation of the good world in which he was set and for the miscarriage of the possibilities provided him for true community. It is high time, therefore, to take seriously the biblical testimony about God's involvement in the human lot made miserable by man's rebellion and to seek a richer understanding of the apostolic faith that, since God *is* love, the essence of his providence is *com*passion.

In such a search we are, of course, stuck with the prime article of Christian belief: that the Maker of heaven and earth wrought well and that the creation even as it stands is a more appropriate matrix for God's Kingdom than any other alternative. From this it follows that if human freedom and love are the chief agencies in the ruination of the human enterprise, then freedom and love rightly used must indeed be values of such ultimate concern that God Almighty deliberately risked a creation like this to make them possible. In this sense, it *is* the best of all possible worlds, *for what God had in mind.* In his forbearance of the havoc wrought by freedom and love abused, his ways *are* past finding out—unless there is some hope of the entire venture ever being seen steadily and whole. All the alternatives—save atheism —are blasphemous: that he could have done better and didn't, that he tried and failed, that love and hate are equally ultimate, that the God who does not "intervene" also couldn't care less. Better atheism than any of these. The atheist, of course, has a different problem. Given the human abuse of freedom (or any other etiology of misery) what is *his* ground for any hope at all that such men can rightwise their own existence and achieve their true possibilities within *his* terms of reference? Here, obviously, the burden of overbelief shifts to the other side.

The Christian hope springs from the faith that the providence of the *possibilities and potencies* in this creation is sufficient for the triumph of God's good purposes in the optimum realization of human blessedness. In this sense, what God made and goes on making is *good;* even in its corruption, the residues of created good remain. It would then follow that the miscarriages of some of these good possibilities are the shadow side of the possibility for the realizations of others. Our misery is an ironic testimony to the fact of our awareness that blessedness is the goal for which human existence was originally designed. And if the question arises as to whether God was just or wise in making us free if being free would make us miserable, we then stand on the threshold of the biblical insight that God's "justice" is not so much a matter of his enforcing the law as of his insisting on our freedom—and of his reconciling us even in our offenses against the law by grace *alone* (i.e. freely and for love). This is the gist of the classical doctrine of "justification." Having made us free, and also liable to abuse that freedom, God engages himself in the hazards of our invested freedom—and so provides the way for freedom, abused, to be converted to its proper use for our good and his glory.

The Christian Gospel is the good news that in this world just as it is, and in our lives just as they are, the possibility of God's righteous rule in our hearts and lives is always a live option (". . . and Jesus came preaching, the Kingdom of God is *at hand"* [cf. Matt. 4:17, 10:7; Mark 1:15]). This is what the world is for: to be the arena in which God's righteousness becomes man's blessedness. This is what our lives are for: to receive the Kingdom through Christ its bearer and to share with him the love of the father in the Holy Spirit. This is

the secret hidden for long ages and through many generations, but now disclosed to God's people, to whom it was his will to make it known—to make known how rich and glorious is his grace among all nations. The secret is this: Christ in your midst, the hope of glory! [Col. 1:26-27, NEB]

To know this is to know that our lives are in his hands and that he is in the thick of history with us, providing the potentials of meaningful experience and yet refusing either to coerce or to bless us without our own participation. Here he is in our existence —working, suffering, loving, enduring the indignities of our rebellion and sin as we do—not because he is weak but because he is loving, not because he needs our aid to help him win but because our lives require a climate of divine compassion in order to come to their flower and fruit. Love is redemptive only when it is intimate enough to be personal, unselfish enough to be truly trustworthy. The Passion of Christ did *not* end at Golgotha: it goes on and on to the end of the world, wherever the passions of men go unredeemed. The sacrifice of Calvary is endlessly efficacious, not as a substitute for the sacrifices to which love calls us, but as a purgation of our sacrificial love from self-pity and bitterness. God-with-us: in life's turmoils and drudgery, its vigils and sunbursts, unravelling and reweaving the strands of our memories and hopes, judging, thwarting, leaving us to suffer for our own misdeeds and those of others and yet never forsaking us even in our sufferings. God-with-us: not to dominate but to bless and yet also to prevent the *final* triumph of our resistance to his righteous rule. God-with-us: endlessly patient, endlessly concerned, endlessly resourceful. Here in the biblical secret of Immanuel, the Provident Mystery of God is "present" in the very same projects to which he has assigned us, concerned above all that our experiences come to their created potential. This, or something like it, is faith's answer to the problem of evil.

Even so, the test of such a conviction comes only in the cumulative experience of trustful living—of having our trials and tribulations recognized as the temperings of faith, of being exposed to the strains and torque of the moral conflict in which love is offered and repudiated or corrupted but not withdrawn, of plumbing the heights and depths of joy and sorrow, rejoicing and mourning, glowing health and searing pain, holy and unholy living, the fear of death and the hope of holy dying. These are the "proofs" of God's providence that come finally to be believed and trusted.

What cannot be borne by any man aware of his human dignity—and the dignity of others—is meaningless, wasted, useless life. What we cannot endure is the fear that evil has the final word at life's end. A world in which senseless disasters and catastrophes occur all too often can still be lived in, courageously and grace-fully, *if* the lives affected can be seen, or can be believed, to have finally significant meaning, here and hereafter. Meaningless pain or active cruelty are simply outrageous and destructive of morally meaningful faith. But pain that comes with fruitful travail or useful service may not only be borne but be ennobling. Illness can crumple our morale, or it can be lived with in the light of the instrumental value we attach to health as an agency of our humanity. Heroism is mostly a matter of a man caring more greatly for something other than himself—or caring for himself as the servant of some other value that ranks higher on his scale than his own self-interest.

As a man learns to live in such a spirit—if only fitfully and imperfectly—he comes more and more to appreciate and reach out for the communion of those who have found life good and are devoted to making it good for others, he gains more and more compassion for those whose painful struggles or sodden apathy are equally unavailing. In such an odyssey, God's presence is our ward against loneliness, lostness, and that immoderate love of what has been that dulls our taste for what more there is to come that we may share in. Life becomes more grace-filled and thus more graceful—and the confidence of our trust confirmed and strengthened. And all this, mind you, springs from a "theology of the Cross"!

For those whose lives have begun to be hid with God in Christ, the query about evil gets to be less urgent than what the good is in the situation at hand—and how the provident presence of grace opens up new futures with new meanings that can redeem the bitter residues of past estrangements. The ground for our belief that the battle is worth our best is not that God is above it calling the shots, but that he is *in* it sharing the blows—*and that he is going to win it,* for us men and for our salvation! *Christus Victor* is not our fairy godmother—nor the immutable, impassible Absolute whose relations with creation are non-reciprocal. He is, rather, the author of our salvation, the pioneer of God's providence for our destiny, the power of love that reconciles.[7]

The genius of Christian faith is the learning by living that evil, both physical and moral, is bad (and to be avoided and resisted) but that evil is not invincible and we can reject its claim to have the final word in our lives and others. The solid core of all damnation is the false persuasion that we are done for, that the powers of sin and death have no match, that despair is an honest reading of existence. What we need to know is that all the power wielded by "the powers of sin and death" is actually supplied *by us* in our sin, pride, and fear, as we feed the lie that evil has the upper hand.

It is our Christian calling to fight against all the ills and woes that afflict mankind and against their human causes and provocations. To leave misery unalleviated, to leave social revolution to the angry and selfish, to stand aloof from the agonies of the new world a-borning is to make it all too plain that we are not interested in the compassion of God but only in our own passive hope of his impassible providence. The unanimous "answer" by the saints and heroes of the faith to the problem of evil is disconcertingly simple: evil is overcome by the intelligent, competent concern of people willing to pay the price of conflict. This seems the wrong answer for those of us who think we could devise a better world where all was joy and bliss. But there it is—and its truth can only be verified by the ventures of that Christian gallantry that does not seek pain but rather undertakes to reduce it, that labors with no guidelines save need and opportunity, that does not have to foresee the distant scene in order to know where the action is here and now.

God's providence is his provident presence in all the exigencies of creation. This is never more meaningful than his presence in the anguish of guilt and self-reproach. Here, his grace is to be seen in his pro-vision for the efficacy of repentance and pardon,

---

7. Cf. Col 1: 19-27.

on the one hand, and for the strength of comfort and hope, on the other. Repentance is neither grovelling nor flip remorse; it is the honest recognition of one's own capacity for sin and one's utter need of grace to bear the consequences of sin and to fend off temptation. Pardon is neither a cancelling of the past nor the condonation of evil, but the affirmation of love where wrath was expected and a newly opened future where guilt had foreseen only punishment.

By the same token, "comfort" is not an easement of the demand for righteousness nor a smoothing of the upward way. *Con-fortare* means to offer strength by *standing beside* someone in need of strength. God does not leave us to go it alone, but then neither does he carry any but "the *young* lambs in his bosom." He summons the rest of us to stand on our own feet, to take responsibility for our freedom and its entail—assuring us of needful strength that comes from his standing with and for us. Hope is not the projection of our wishes onto the calendar of the forthcoming future. It is, rather, the confidence that God is holding that future open so that its potential for meaningful participation will remain, so that life will still be fit for living and dying, secure in God's provident presence in life and death and destiny.

Chapter Two

A WORLD WITHOUT SUFFERING

JOHN HICK

To relate the sad facts of human misery to the problem of theodicy, we have to ask ourselves whether a world from which suffering was excluded would serve the divine purpose of "soul-making." Having been created through the long evolutionary process as a personal creature made in the "image" of God, would man be able to grow without suffering towards the finite "likeness" of God?

So far as human nature itself is concerned, the question concerns man's liability to bring suffering upon himself and upon his fellows by his own selfishness, greed, cruelty, and lovelessness. In order for man to be endowed with the freedom in relation to God that is essential if he is to come to his Creator in uncompelled faith and love, he must be initially set at an epistemic "distance" from that Creator. This entails his immersion in an apparently autonomous environment which presents itself to him *etsi deus non daretur,* "as if there were no God." When man is so circumstanced, it is not only possible for him to center his life upon himself rather than upon God, but that it is virtually inevitable that he will do so. Man's "fallenness" is thus the price paid for his freedom as a personal being in relation to the personal Infinite. God is so overwhelmingly great that the children in His heavenly family must be prodigal children who have voluntarily come to their Father from a far country, prompted by their own need and drawn by His love. This means that the sinfulness from which man is being redeemed, and the human suffering which flows from that sinfulness, have in their own paradoxical way a place within the divine providence. Their place, however, is not that of something that ought to exist but of something that ought to be abolished. The contribution which sin and its attendant suffering make to God's plan does not consist in any value intrinsic to themselves but, on the contrary, in the activities whereby they are overcome, namely redemption from sin, and men's mutual service amid suffering.

Given, then, that man must be free—free to center his life upon himself and so to bring suffering upon both himself and others—what does this imply concerning the nature of our environment? In discussing the possibility of a world without pain, such an anaesthetic existence would lack the stimuli to hunting, agriculture, and building, social organization, and to the development of the sciences and technologies, which have been essential foci of human civilization and culture. If we expand further the notion of a painless world into one in which there is no suffering of any kind, we shall find that the integral character of the present order entails that more would be lost even than civilization and culture.

We may follow David Hume as our guide to a world devoid of pain and suffering, and continue the discussion arising out of his second complaint concerning the universe. He makes here two suggestions, one more and one less radical. The more radical one is this: "Might not the Deity exterminate all ill, wherever it were to be found; and produce all good, without any preparation or long progress of causes and effects?"[1] In other words, might not

---

1. **Dialogues Concerning Natural Religion,** pt. xi, Kemp-Smith's ed., Oxford: Clarendon Press, 1935, p. 253.

God directly intervene in the workings of nature to prevent any occasion of suffering and to produce a maximum of pleasure and happiness?

The initial answer is of course that God, being omnipotent, could do this. But let us imagine Hume's suggested policy being carried out, noting in particular its consequences for man's status as a moral being. It would mean that no wrong action could ever have bad effects, and that no piece of carelessness or ill judgment in dealing with the world could ever lead to harmful consequences. If a thief were to steal a million pounds from a bank, instead of anyone being made poorer thereby, another million pounds would appear from nowhere to replenish the robbed safe; and this, moreover, without causing any inflationary consequences. If one man tried to murder another, his bullet would melt innocuously into thin air, or the blade of his knife turn to paper. Fraud, deceit, conspiracy, and treason would somehow always leave the fabric of society undamaged. Anyone driving at breakneck speed along a narrow road and hitting a pedestrian would leave his victim miraculously unharmed; or if one slipped and fell through a fifth-floor window, gravity would be partially suspended and he would float gently to the ground. And so on. We can at least begin to imagine a world custom-made for the avoidance of all suffering. But the daunting fact that emerges is that in such a world qualities would no longer have any point or value. There would be nothing wrong with stealing, because no one could ever lose anything by it; there would be no such crime as murder, because no one could ever be killed; and in short none of the terms connoting modes of injury—such as cruelty, treachery, deceit, neglect, assault, injustice, unfaithfulness—would retain its meaning. If to act wrongly means, basically, to harm someone, there would no longer be any such thing as morally wrong action. And for the same reason there would no longer be any such thing as morally right action. Not only would there be no way in which anyone could injure anyone else, but there would also be no way in which anyone could benefit anyone else, since there would be no possibility of any lack or danger. It would be a world without need for the virtues of self-sacrifice, care for others, devotion to the public good, courage, perseverance, skill, or honesty. It would indeed be a world in which such qualities, having no function to perform, would never come into existence. Unselfishness would never be evoked in a situation in which no one was ever in real need or danger. Honesty, good faith, commitment to the right would never be evoked in circumstances in which no one could ever suffer any harm, so that there were no bad consequences of dishonesty, bad faith, or moral vacillation. Courage would never be evoked in an environment devoid of all dangers; determination and persistence would never be evoked in the absence of any challenges and obstacles. Truthfulness would never be evoked in a world in which to tell a lie never had any ill effects. And so on. Perhaps most important of all, the capacity to love would never be developed, except in a very limited sense of the word, in a world in which there was no such thing as suffering. The most mature and valuable form of love in human life is the love between a man and a woman upon which the family is built. This love is not a merely physical or a purely romantic enjoyment of each other, although that is where it begins and that should always be an element within it. But it can grow into something more than this, namely a joint facing of the task of creating a home together and the bearing of one another's burdens through all the length of a lifetime. Such love perhaps expresses itself most fully in mutual giving and helping and sharing in times of difficulty.[2]

---

2. As James Hinton argued in his classic meditation on the mystery of pain, "We could never have felt the joy, never had even the idea, of love, if sacrifice had been impossible to us." (**The Mystery of Pain,** 1866, London: Hodder & Stoughton, 1911, p. 51.) Cf. Josiah Royce: "Even love shows its glory as love only by its conquest over the doubts and estrangements, the absences and the misunderstandings, the griefs and the loneliness, that love glorifies with its light amidst all their tragedy." (**The World and the Individual,** New York: Macmillan, 1901, vol. ii, p. 409). Royce presented his own idealist theodicy here and in "The problem of Job" (Studies in Good and Evil, 1898, reprinted in Walter Kaufmann, ed., **Religion from Tolstoy to Camus,** New York: Harper & Row, 1961).

And it is hard to see how such love could ever be developed in human life, in this its deepest and most valuable form of mutual caring and sharing, except in an environment that has much in common with our own world. It is, in particular, difficult to see how it could ever grow to any extent in a paradise that excluded all suffering. For such love presupposes a "real life" in which there are obstacles to be overcome, tasks to be performed, goals to be achieved, setbacks to be endured, problems to be solved, dangers to be met; and if the world did not contain the particular obstacles, difficulties, problems, and dangers that it does contain, then it would have to contain others instead. The same is true in relation to the virtues of compassion, unselfishness, courage, and determination—these all presuppose for their emergence and for their development something like the world in which we live. They are values of personal existence that would have no point, and therefore no place, in a ready-made Utopia. And therefore, if the purpose for which this world exists (so far as that purpose concerns mankind) is to be a sphere within which such personal qualities are born, to purge it of all suffering would be a sterile reform.

At the same time, it is to be noted that we have, in all this, discerned only a very general connection between the kind of world in which we are living and the development of so many of the more desirable qualities of human personality. We have seen that, from our human point of view, this is a world with rough edges, a place in which man can live only by the sweat of his brow, and which continually presents him with challenges, uncertainties, and dangers; and yet that just these features of the world seem, paradoxically, to underlie the emergence of virtually the whole range of the more valuable human characteristics.

Chapter Three

THE SON OF MAN MUST SUFFER

The title "Son of Man" is used in the gospels of Jesus by himself,
not by others. Outside of the gospels the title occurs once in Acts
and twice in the Apocalypse. The title is obscure in English,
and it was obscure in Greek; this seems to be the reason why it
was not employed outside the Palestinian church, if the New Testament usage is any key to its frequency. No other title of Jesus has
been submitted to such a searching examination, and it is not
to our purpose here to relate the divergent conclusions which have
been reached. For our purpose it is sufficient to notice that in the
New Testament this title was Jesus's favorite designation of himself,
and that it was original with him. When we attempt to trace earlier
uses of the title, we run into difficulties.

"Son of Man" renders literally a Hebrew and Aramaic phrase
which signifies an individual member of the human species; the
Hebrew and Aramaic words translated by "man" are collective
nouns, like the English "cattle," and something must be added
to designate the individual. The added word is "son" for a male
and "daughter" for a female. As a pure matter of semantics, the
phrase could be rendered "the man" or "this man," and could be,

when one uses it of oneself, a polite circumlocution for the personal pronoun. Yet no interpreter of the gospels thinks this is all the phrase means. It has overtones which are difficult to analyze.

The uses of the title in the gospels fall into three classes. The first class includes those passages which allude to the second coming of the Son of Man. This use does not concern us here, interesting as it is. The second class is used with reference to what we may call the human condition of Jesus; here the title is linked with some feature of his humanity, either his community with mankind in such things as eating and drinking, or the incarnational character of his mission exhibited in such activities as speech or miracles. The third class includes passages in which the title is associated with the passion and death of Jesus. This third class is really a specific group within the second class, for nowhere is the humanity of Jesus more manifest than in his passion and death.

Doubts about the genuine humanity of Jesus were one of the oldest heresies, probably as old as the New Testament writings. The Church dealt much more solemnly and much more frequently with doubts about his divinity; but the doubts about his humanity have been more subtle and more persistent. The name given to this ancient heresy is docetism; the name is derived from a Greek word, and defines the heresy as the doctrine that Jesus only seemed to be human. In the extreme forms of the heresy, the incarnation was a vast optical illusion or a vast pantomine. In the more subtle forms of the heresy, Christians whose belief is otherwise orthodox hesitate to attribute to Jesus those aspects of the human condition which are in more refined societies thought gross or unseemly. Jesus, it is felt, could not have engaged himself in the human condition to a depth which a cultivated lady or gentleman would find beneath their dignity. But Jesus himself preferred a title which emphasized his common humanity; as for his dignity, he put himself in the position of lackey and was charged with preferring low company, a charge which he cheerfully accepted.[1]

---

1. Mt 9: 10-13; Mk. 2: 13-17; Lk 5: 27-32.

A phrase occurs in Jesus's predictions of his passion: "The Son of Man must suffer."[2] It is intriguing that if this sentence is lifted from its context, the Aramaic phrase permits the translation "Man must suffer." In submission to suffering, Jesus did nothing which distinguishes his own condition from the general human condition; for suffering belongs to the general human condition. Our task here is not to discuss why this is so; we are satisfied with the fact. Two of the great systems of ancient Greek philosophy, stoicism and epicureanism, built their morality around man's response to pleasure and pain, and many thinkers since have dealt with the problem—as a rule, not too successfully. No one can expect to live without at some time experiencing sharp physical and mental pain. When this happens, one is aware of the loneliness of pain. No matter how much compassion and kindly ministration one receives, there is a block to communication. Others cannot share the pain, even if they have suffered similar pain themselves. The voices of one's friends seem to come from a great distance, too great for one to hear or answer them clearly. One feels low, even de-humanized; one is ashamed of one's weakness and self-pity. It is at this point, of course, that one doubts that Jesus ever suffered as we do. He must have had some hidden resource which made his suffering less degrading. It may take a little thought to see that ideas of this kind are disrespectful to him; in a way they challenge his honesty.

When we think of the suffering of Jesus, we think first of his passion; and possibly we think of nothing else. We think of the passion, perhaps, as an exquisite and prolonged agony of physical and mental pain, beyond anything endured by ordinary man. In fact, the passion of Jesus, like so much of his life, was commonplace in the world in which he lived. The Hellenistic-Roman world was civilized, but it was harsh in war and in the administration of law. It did not notably exceed in harshness the later European world until quite recent times; and indeed one may ask whether the modern European world has entirely risen above bar-

---

2. Mk 8: 31; Lk 9: 22.

barism in these areas. Our own generation is no stranger to the cruelty of man to man. The death inflicted upon Jesus was a routine punishment for certain types of crime. Appalling as it seems to us, and its cruelty was recognized in ancient times also, it was not an unusual punishment.

Nor is there any reason to think that Jesus was unusually delicate and sensitive to pain. As he is described in the gospels, there is ample reason to think that he was not. The average man of those times seems to have been less well nourished and less well developed in physique than modern civilized man; but the peasant had a sturdy body which was accustomed to prolonged physical exertion and lack of adequate food. There was no comfort in his life, and some things he could endure better than we can. The weak did not survive infancy; those who did survive were those who could resist disease and infection and who did not tire quickly. We should not take anything away from the pains of the passion of Jesus, but he could stand them better than most of us could stand them. Violent death at the hands of one's fellow-men was a more common risk in that world than it has yet become in ours; and I suspect that the mental attitude of the ancient man towards this hazard was not much different from our own quite casual acceptance of the risks of the motor car.

A difficulty in studying the response of Jesus to pain is that the gospels are extremely objective narratives. They never get into the minds of the people who appear in them, neither into the mind of Jesus nor of any one else. They relate the external signs of thought and emotion. If the ancient Near East was anything like the modern Near East, emotions were disclosed with a candor which the modern European finds embarrassing. The passion narratives tell us nothing of the response of Jesus to the passion. We have only the account of Gethsemane, which tells us that the anticipation of the passion was so entirely human that, as I have remarked, the modern European finds it embarrassing. I have read numerous homiletic expositions of Gethsemane which attempted to plumb some mystical depths of Jesus which caused him such exquisite anguish that it burst forth in his behavior. That Jesus should have quailed at the anticipation of pain is something these writers cannot bring themselves to say. It would be too human; but it is not sinful. No doubt there were mystical depths in this experience which the gospels do not relate, and which it might be impudent to attempt to analyze; but the behavior of Jesus in this crisis needs no such explanation. What might need explanation is the composure which the gospels describe in him after the agony of Gethsemane. Here is seen a man who is well aware of the pain involved in his decision, but who has refused to allow the pain to divert him from his course, or even to force him to show any weakness. In some way we manage to make this composure the result of something else than a tremendous effort of will. When we think of Jesus as being above emotional pressure, we also think of him as being above character.

The mental pain of the passion can only be deduced from the narrative; we can guess some of it, but no doubt the homilists are right in believing that there is more here than we can reach. The Gethsemane narrative shows clearly that Jesus was as well acquainted with the loneliness of pain as anyone of us. That his mental pain could not be shared with any one is easily deduced; for no one else knew the issues involved. That he should have sought the mere presence of others at this time ought to be revealing. It is not a pleasure to feel the violent hatred of others, and to know that there are people who are convinced that your death will make the world a better place to live in. It is likewise no pleasure to know that those who are closest to you seem completely unaware of the weight which you carry. When this happens to us, we call it our private hell.

We noticed above that when we think of the suffering which Jesus endured as Son of Man, we are likely to concentrate on the passion so intensely that we do not notice other things in the gospels. These other things should not be exaggerated; in the preceding paragraphs it will be thought by some readers that I have worked too diligently to reduce the passion of Jesus to the commonplace. To a degree this is true; for unless the sufferings of Jesus are something like our own, I do not see how his experience of suffering can be meaningful for us. If he was made of some super-flesh which was insensitive to pain, or if he was endowed with a super-soul which served as an anaesthetic, he would not really share our sufferings. The community which he has with us may be more easily observed in other episodes which are obviously nearer to the commonplace.

The life of Jesus as described in the gospels does not appear to be one prolonged and uninterrupted agony of pain. He does not appear as the wealthy nobleman who is compelled to spend some years in the pigsty. Distressing as it may be, when he dealt with Palestinian peasants he dealt with his own kind of people, the people with whom he was most at home; and I fear that delicate is one of the last words we can apply to him. There is no reason to delay on the quality of Palestinian village life, since a certain crudeness was truthfully commonplace in Palestinian villages. Such things as primitive and crowded housing (or frequently no housing), sub-standard nourishment, a working day of twelve hours or more, a total absence of anything we would call amusement or recreation, a wardrobe of a cloak and a tunic, constant harassment by one's betters, day to day subsistence on the margin of destitution: these were the life of the villager, and the villager would not count them among his sufferings. Here Jesus seemed to fare no better and no worse than his class. But it seems legitimate to conclude that he was also familiar with the few simple pleasures which belonged to the villager, and that he appreciated them. The villager is both clannish and gregarious; he enjoys the company of his own, and in the almost total lack of privacy in the village it is better that he should enjoy it. Nothing in the gospels suggests that Jesus did not enjoy his human associations; at least nothing indicates that he was ever thought withdrawn. The many illustrations drawn both from the Palestinian landscape and from the life of the Palestinian villager show again that Jesus knew this life and that he appreciated it. In these illustrations, both in and out of the parables, he spoke to the people he knew about the things they both knew. In the traditions of ancient Near-Eastern wisdom, the wise man was he who could draw a profound lesson from familiar sights and objects. All these things suggest that Jesus was thoroughly integrated with the world in which he lived, and that he enjoyed life up to its full capacity.

Within this village life, however, Jesus was an exceptional figure. This we easily conclude. It was not merely that he was a rabbi—at least that was the term which best identified him; this caused no concern except that he taught without having been a disciple. But we are puzzled that the villagers did not seem to grasp the fact that he was exceptional. This, apparently, was grasped only by those who became his dedicated enemies. His exceptional mission created problems, and several times his words refer to this inevitable result of his mission.[3] They are the problems in human relations created by one who departs from conformity, who refuses to accept the conventions and acts to change them. We have already mentioned that it is no pleasure to be the object of hatred. No one can enjoy this except one who has achieved a kind of congealed self-righteousness. The self-righteous man can enjoy being hated because he can return it with such a good conscience. Self-righteous is not a word which can be applied to Jesus. That he was indifferent to hatred is an illegitimate assumption. That he was unfeeling at the knowledge that he was the object of a campaign of calumny is impossible unless people meant nothing to him. The worst construction was put upon his words and actions. The gospels describe a vigilant espionage and an unremitting whispering campaign which effectively tore down most of what he built.

At the risk of knocking off some plaster, it must be noticed that Jesus responded to this hostility with feeling; and this is a sure sign that it penetrated.[4] The exchanges between Jesus and hostile groups are not conducted on a high level of politeness; we are, as we have noticed, in the villages of Palestine, and in these villages insults are not veiled. "Whited sepulchres" and "brood of vipers" are somewhat stylized in the English Bible, but they are not flattering, and they certainly do not meet the standards of etiquette of parliamentary debate. They betray the fact that the person who uses them has been hurt, which is more or less the

---

3. Mt 10: 34-36; Lk 12: 51-53.
4. Mt 12: 1-4, 34; 15: 1-20; 28: 1-39; Mk 2: 23—3, 6; 7: 1-23; Lk 6: 1-11, 11: 37-52.

point we are trying to make. Again the reaction of Jesus is normal.

The relations of Jesus with his disciples furnish another insight into the pains which arose from the mission of Jesus. Most modern commentators on the gospels believe that the Galilean ministry of Jesus, which seems to have occupied the greater part of his public life, issued in no large and deep penetration into the popular mind. Measured in terms of numbers of adherents gained, the mission was a failure. The point may be argued, but it is not necessary for our purpose to discuss it. If we turn our attention to the effect of the words of Jesus on that group which was closest to him, which he had chosen as his disciples, which had more opportunity to grasp his message than anyone else, the picture of a large band of understanding and devoted followers is difficult to maintain. If such a large band existed, then his chosen group must have come from that element among his listeners which had understood him least. The dullness of the disciples is quite clear in Mark, so clear that both Matthew and Luke have softened it somewhat. There can be no doubt that the picture of Mark is more original, for Matthew and Luke have preserved many of the sayings and conversations in which the dullness of the disciples is manifest.

Here, as in the disputes with the Pharisees, we see that Jesus responded to the situation with feeling.[5] The disciples are called slow-witted, stupid and unbelieving, and on one classic occasion their leading personality is said to be on the side of the devil and not of God.[6] In anyone else such language would be an expression of impatience. Let us at least say that Jesus knew the movement which grips one who has spent much time and labor on something which he believes is important, only to have it ignored or frustrated by simple mindlessness. This again is no pleasure; indeed, it is one of life's keener disappointments, and in some instances it can reach almost tragic dimensions. If Jesus was above such movements of feeling, the gospels do not suggest it. His reaction to the disciples is vigorous, scarcely less vigorous

---

5. Mt 15: 15; 16: 5-11; 17: 20; Mk 7: 18; 8: 14-21.
6. Mt 16: 23; Mk 8: 33.

than his reaction to the Pharisees. After all, he had reason to expect more from the disciples; and we all know that those who are closest to us can hurt us more than those who are remote.

We have remarked above that the candid expression of emotion is characteristic of the simple culture; the more refined culture believes that public or even private display of strong emotion should be restrained. This restraint seems to the simple peasant to be not restraint but insensibility. Because the gospels arise from a simple culture, neither Jesus nor any one else is often said to manifest emotion; the listeners could assume that emotion was shown. Rarely is Jesus said to weep, never is he said to laugh, rarely is a word used which suggests a movement of anger.[7] The most candid passage under this heading is the Gethsemane narrative. Jesus is never described in terms which suggest that he was unfeeling or unresponsive. No doubt we are correct in attributing to him a fine emotional balance which never permitted his emotions to go out of control; but we are much less surely correct in thinking that his behavior exhibited what we consider emotional balance and control. If he was an authentic villager—and nothing indicates that he was not—when he felt pain it could be easily discerned.

Here also we may appear to be reducing the sufferings of Jesus to the commonplace; and again in a sense we are. When we talk about these problems in personal relations, we are talking about a fact of common experience; and the unique quality of the person and mission of Jesus does not make the problem any less common. Such personal problems can range from minor irritations to motives for murder. They form a major portion of our lives. It is rare that we are exposed to great danger or to intense pain; what passes for suffering in our lives is not so intense that we live in a constant emotional crisis. At the same time, we rarely know moments of complete emotional repose. This is exactly the picture of Jesus which the gospels give us. The picture, as we have said, is not of a man who feels no pain, who is so far above pain that he does not deign to notice it, but of a man who, however keenly

7. Mk 3: 5.

he feels it, does not allow it to affect his decisions and his course of action. And, as we observed in speaking of the passion, we seem reluctant to attribute this to the power of will. We are ready to grant the will-power of Jesus, but we have our doubts about the power of his emotions.

In all of this there appears no cult of pain and suffering for their own sake. Jesus assures his disciples that they will experience pain by following him.[8] To take up the cross was a figure of speech which had a quite different impact in the first century from the impact it has in the twentieth, when a "cross" may be anything from an incurable cancer to rain on a picnic. Jesus does not suggest that his disciples should seek pain; he rather makes it clear that if they remain disciples they will not have to seek it, it will seek them. He nowhere demands that they should submit to pain with more restraint than he showed himself. They need not make themselves unfeeling. What they must not do is let suffering divert them from their commitments. Suffering is a temptation just as pleasure is a temptation; and it is a question whether deliberately cultivated suffering is any less a temptation than deliberately culti-vated pleasure. It is not impossible that the disciple might choose a deliberately cultivated tolerable pain in preference to the incal-culable pain which is risked by the full commitment of discipleship.

A consideration of the attitude of Jesus towards his own suffer-ing would be incomplete without some reference to his attitude towards the suffering of others. Here brevity is in order, for no one has ever doubted the compassion of Jesus for his fellow men. We may not always realize how deeply this compassion was rooted in a sharing of the common unglamorous suffering of man-kind, and it has been our purpose to emphasize this point. Jesus has no quick cure for suffering, and he does not promise a world in which there will be no suffering; nothing but the coming of the reign of God will bring this to pass. Nor does he present any rationalization of suffering; after the gospel, as before, suffering is still one of the great irrational factors in human life. Jesus shows how one can live with it, not how one can think it out of

---

8. Mt 10: 17-39; Mk 13: 9-13; Lk 21: 12-17.

existence. Indeed he shows more, for it is by this very human condition that man, incorporated in Christ, will rise to a new life. All of these are rather obvious theological statements; but they do not change the fact that Jesus showed compassion. We have no record of his saying to anyone in pain, "But it is so good for you."

We turn to the parables, which show so much awareness of the importance of the little things in life. We see the anguish of a woman so poor that she must sweep the whole house to find a lost coin.[9] We share the weariness of the shepherd who finds at the end of the day that his count shows one missing sheep.[10] We learn of the bewildered desperation of the husbandman who sees that his wheat crop turns out to be mostly weeds.[11] We have the shocking contrast of the starving beggar dying at the door of a man who eats to his heart's content.[12] We are told of the man who lies robbed and bleeding in the ditch, and sees those who could help him pass on their way.[13] We hear of the sheer terror of the man who is hopelessly in debt with no way out.[14] We have a vivid picture of men whose livelihood is the wage of the day, standing in the market place from dawn through most of the afternoon, and there is no work for them.[15] These are not the human tragedies of which great literature is made. But they are the stuff of life, the life which Jesus knew and could describe with feeling which is apparent in the somewhat sober prose of the gospels.

The compassion of Jesus is luminously evident in the miracle stories. These are almost without exception accounts of how Jesus dealt with individual existing problems of suffering. The gospels here present him as the person in whom the reign of God enters the world and moves against the powers of sin and death. Suffering

---

9. Lk 15: 8-9.
10. Mt 18: 12-13; Lk 15: 3-6.
11. Mt 13: 24-30.
12. Lk 16: 19-22.
13. Lk 10: 30-31.
14. Mt 18: 23-30.
15. Mt 20: 1-6.

belongs to the reign of sin and death, and suffering cannot be attacked unless its roots are attacked. When Jesus is asked to cure a paralytic he first forgives sins; the theological implications are apparent, and no explanation is necessary.[16] Several times also he expresses simple human compassion for a fellow human being who is in pain. He is indignant at the Pharisees who believe that a woman who has been crippled for eighteen years can wait one more day for a cure until the Sabbath rest is ended.[17] The anger of Jesus at this point is most revealing, for if the question is weighed in the scale of absolutes the complaint of the Pharisees is quite reasonable. The Sabbath is important, and one day does not seem to add much to eighteen years. Yet it is the sheer reasonableness of the pharisaic position which angers Jesus. This is to put things before persons, to treat human suffering as a calculable factor—in short, to use it. When people are suffering, there is no reasonable cause for delay which can be urged.

The same theme appears in stories of the disputes of Jesus with the Pharisees concerning the Sabbath observance. He allows the Sabbath to interfere with no human need, even if the need be small. When the disciples nibbled at the raw grain in the fields, there is no doubt they were hungry; modern civilized man rarely if ever experiences the perpetual hunger of the poor. But they were not, in the terms of their own life, starving; nevertheless, the pettiness of the pharisaic observance again arouses the anger of Jesus. Such an attitude shows more interest in the welfare of draught animals than in the welfare of people.[18]

Nothing drew more severe words from Jesus, words in which anger is evident, than words and actions which bring suffering to others.[19] Scarcely less severity is shown to indifference to human suffering which one has not actively caused; we are reminded of the parable of Dives and Lazarus, in which the rich man is damned for literally doing nothing. Perhaps this particular species of moral fault should be more prominently listed in our catalogues

---

16. Mt 9: 2-7; Mk 2: 1-12; Lk 5: 17-26.
17. Lk 13: 10-17.
18. Mt 12: 1-8; Mk 2: 23-27; Lk 6: 1-5.
19. Mt 18: 32-34; 23: 4.

of vices. The great test recounted in Matthew is entirely concerned with what one has done or failed to do to alleviate the suffering of others.[20] The more obvious and vicious crimes against the human person do not appear in this list; after all, Jesus is speaking to his disciples, and it could be presumed that they had learned some basic lessons which were taught in Judaism. But they had not learned what this passage tells them, that if they have committed no crime against their neighbor, it is still not enough. The failure here is simply the failure to take action against suffering when one encounters it; and this lesson can still be proclaimed in the Church.

Let us sum up if we can these scattered reflections. Our emphasis has been less on the great and the tragic sufferings in the life of Jesus and more on the commonplace in his sufferings. It is in the commonplace rather than in the great and tragic that we are more aware of his community with us. In his sufferings we discern the gospel theme that suffering is a part of the reign of sin and death; it is evil, not good, and the heart of the mystery of our redemption is that we are saved through something which is involved with sin and death. The gospel does not require us to praise suffering or to affirm that it has a goodness which it does not have. Suffering is a part of the human condition, that condition which in biblical language is called a curse.

We observe that Jesus was neither unusually sensitive to suffering nor unusually insensitive, as far as we can deduce from the gospels. We observe that the Christian attitude does not require an unfeeling response to suffering. Jesus responded emotionally not only to the great and tragic suffering of his passion, but also to the lesser pains of life. We have paid particular attention to this where the pains are the result either of the malice or of the thoughtlessness of others; for do not our own sufferings come mostly from these? And in the last analysis, we suffer far more from the thoughtlessness of others than we do from their malice. In both instances we see that Jesus let people know what they were doing, and let them know that he did not like it. I am not sure that

---

20. Mt 25: 31-46.

calm acceptance is altogether the apt phrase to describe this attitude. One may, and no doubt will, distinguish his response to merely personal suffering and to the suffering involved in his mission; but to others this distinction will be meaningless.

Yet this is the same Jesus who tells us that the greatest christian act is the love of one's enemies; and unless his life was altogether inconsistent, we must believe that this reaction to hostility and stupidity was not inconsistent with love. We often fear that such a reaction is inconsistent with love; yet is it love to permit people to inflict pain on others? One might argue that the gospels make very little difference between inflicting pain and permitting its infliction. We have observed that it is in this area of conduct that Jesus speaks with greatest severity. Whatever be one's attitude towards one's suffering, one is never free, it seems, to be indifferent to the suffering of others. Jesus does not promise that we can create a world free of suffering, but he does seem to expect that we shall deal with it when we meet it as if we could. The Christian's response to the suffering of others is scarcely more tolerant than his response to sin.

The Christian can do something with suffering which he cannot do with sin, and that is to take it from others upon himself. This is what we believe that Jesus himself did, and we believe that he empowered us to do it. In fact he offers no other solution to the problem of suffering in the world. Christians may ask both the Church and themselves how much this power has been exercised in the past and how much it is exercised in the present. One knows that most schemes for a better life and a better world are proposed with little attention given to vicarious suffering. They proceed as if man's suffering had no connection with man's sin, as if we could move against suffering without getting as deeply involved in it as Jesus was; and for that reason one has reservations about their success. When the gospels are read closely and thoughtfully on this question, they appear to be the most practical documents we possess.

Chapter Four

WE REJOICE IN OUR SUFFERINGS

JOSEPH BLENKINSOPP

"Man," as Eliphaz remarked to Job, "is born to trouble as the sparks fly upwards."[1] He cannot avoid it even by remaining completely immobile. He has to put up with it, but if he is a religious man he can hardly avoid reflecting on why God permits it, especially when its incidence is so often apparently casual and arbitrary. For most of the Old Testament suffering is regarded as a passivity, with the emphasis on how the faithful man is to integrate it into his world of inner conviction and cope with it. There was the so-called 'classical' doctrine on suffering according to which its infliction is part of God's moral government of the world, by which he punished sinners and, at the same time, "encourages the others." "Man and boy," says the psalmist, "I have never seen the righteous abandoned nor his descendants having to beg for their bread."[2] Maybe he hadn't, but this would not have been everyone's experience, and as we get further into the Old Testament we can see this view wearing progressively

---

1. Job 5: 7.
2. Ps 37: 25.

thinner. More consistent was the idea that suffering is the lot of all, just and unjust indifferently, but that the just man, by the very fact of his being just, would have the strength of spirit to survive rather than to curse God and die.

Perhaps the most typical Jewish contribution to this attempt to cope with suffering by giving it some intelligibility is the view that suffering is God's way of educating his people. It is the road away from unreality and inauthentic living. The hungering and thirsting in the desert was to lead them to see what man lives by. Suffering is not directly willed by God, but he allows it in order that we may grow strong, as he left the nations in the land of promise for the sake of his people. But even here, suffering is something that merely happens to people; it is not seen as having a positive role.

With the prophetic mission and the opposition which it stirred up, we find a different situation. Here suffering takes on a definite form and features. The clearest case of this is the career of Jeremiah, commissioned to "pluck up and break down, destroy and overthrow."[3] Maybe thinking over the place of suffering in Jeremiah's mission played a part in preparing for the Isaian Servant's mission, which is carried out not in spite of or merely accompanied by suffering, but by means of it. Here we find the roots not just of the peculiar Jewish mystique of suffering but the Christian paradox of fulfillment through suffering, life through death and rejoicing in suffering. And this brings us to Paul.

Paul, in the first place, remains true to the biblical insight of suffering as essential towards authentic living. He lays down the pattern in his Letter to the Romans: "Suffering produces endurance, endurance produces character and character produces hope." [4] This endurance, *hypomone,*[5] is, literally, the quality of a man who remains unmoving and silent beneath the lash. It is a positive endurance of life in the world with all the contrarieties which it brings, a refusal to complain or to seek easy options.

---

3. Jer 1: 10.
4. Rom 5: 3-4.
5. Cf. Walsh, James, 'The Patience of Christ,' **The Way,** Vol. 5, October 1965, p. 293, note 1.

The man who, over a long period has shown this quality of positive endurance, can be said to be approved, *dokimos,* like precious metal tried and purified in the crucible. We should note here that Paul does not provide his Christians with theological alibis for suffering. There is no short cut. The sufferings of life in the world, life as body, are not regarded as illusory, though he will go on to say later that they are not worthy to be compared to the glory that shall be revealed in us.[6] They are not sidestepped by some process of sublimation. Life as it is has to be gone through and not around, lived out, sweated out. It is only when he has reached the stage of approval as a man[7] that the theological virtue of hope is mentioned. There is, moreover, no discontinuity between the real, lived-out experience and the part of God: "... character produces hope, and hope does not disappoint us, because God's love has been poured out into our hearts through the Holy Spirit which has been given to us."[8]

In common with Old Testament prophetic figures like Jeremiah, Paul speaks almost always of suffering within the context of his missionary vocation. The story told in Acts speaks for itself. If we are told that it was an integral part of missionary preaching to the churches of the first hour that "through many tribulations we must enter the kingdom of God,"[9] this is certainly a reflection of experience and, in fact, comes immediately after we read of Paul being stoned and left for dead at Lystra. A little later, in the address on the seashore at Miletus, we read how "the Holy Spirit testifies to me in every city (through prophets like Agabus) that imprisonment and afflictions await me."[10] The catalogue of sufferings enumerated in Paul's well-known *historia calamitatum*[11] deals with the mission, and is set in a context which has to do with establishing his authentic apostolic status. It is not just the constant physical hardship involved but "the daily

---

6. Rom 8: 12 ff.
7. The RSV uses here the word character. Rom 5: 4.
8. Rom 5: 5.
9. Acts 14: 22.
10. Acts 20: 23.
11. 2 Cor 11-12.

pressure upon me of my anxiety for all the churches."[12] The implication is obvious. For the apostle, suffering is inescapable: since he, like Jeremiah, is called to witness to a strange and, for many, unwelcome new presence in the world, he too is commissioned to "pluck up and break down, destroy and overthrow." The words of Jesus in the eschatological discourse of Greek Matthew are, as is generally recognized, the reflection of the missionary experience, a partial chronicle of which is found in Acts: "They will deliver you up to tribulation and put you to death; and you will be hated by all nations for my name's sake."[13] And more specifically: "They will deliver you up to councils and you will be beaten in synagogues."[14] This is precisely what happened to the apostles who were imprisoned and beaten and who, we are told, "left the presence of the council rejoicing that they were counted worthy to suffer dishonor for the Name."[15] Here the suffering is not only borne positively, endured, but rejoiced in. The suffering is part of the enduring witness which issues in the total witness of martyrdom, and martyrdom was the lot of all the apostles, as it was of Paul.

The pattern of apostolic suffering was set, as we saw, in the first missionary tour. It is repeated in the second during which Paul was almost lynched at Philippi, then beaten and imprisoned. It is part of the Christian paradox of suffering with joy that we find the prisoners praying and singing hymns during that long dark and uncomfortable night in a strange town.[16] Signed with the mark of the cross and sealed with the Spirit, they took suffering to be the sign of apostolic authenticity and therefore could rejoice. We should note, moreover, how this also excluded any slightest sign of the self-pity which suffering often induces. On the contrary, Paul preserved the ability to react vigorously by demanding an apology for the indignity inflicted on a Roman citizen and gave an example to all persecuted minorities by con-

---

12. 2 Cor 11: 28.
13. Mt 24: 9.
14. Mt 10: 17.
15. Acts 5: 41.
16. Acts 16: 25.

tinuing to speak out "... though we had already suffered and been shamefully treated at Philippi, as you know, we had confidence in our God to speak out the gospel to you in the face of great opposition."[17]

It was no accident that the main burden of Paul's preaching to the Thessalonians was the necessity of suffering for Christ and the Christian,[18] since this church had received the Word "in much affliction, with joy inspired by the Holy Spirit"[19] and had been instructed from the start on the role of suffering in the building up of the Christian life. For them, as for the first apostles and the "churches of God which are in Judaea," suffering was the mark of those chosen by God, the sign of approval.[20] The consistency of Paul's thinking can be seen in the recurrence, throughout the two letters, of vocabulary elsewhere commonly used in this context, especially the pattern: suffering—endurance—approval—hope. This will remain throughout, but experience will fill out the words with an ever increasing depth of meaning.

In the next stage, at Athens, it seems that Paul experienced a new form of suffering, that of disillusionment, coming to terms with one's own limitations. His first over-optimistic assessment of the apostolic mission to the Gentiles received a hard knock, and he went on to Corinth a bitterly disappointed man. We can assess his state of mind on arrival from the opening chapter of his first letter;[21] though this has no doubt been colored by the even deeper inner darkness in which he was plunged for some time during his three-year mission at Ephesus. It was during this time that the correspondence to the Corinthian church was written: "We do not want you to be ignorant, brethren, of the affliction we experienced in Asia; for we were so utterly, unbearably crushed that we despaired of life itself. Why, we had received the sentence of death; but that was to make us rely not on ourselves but on God who raises the dead."[22] For a man of Paul's

17. 1 Thess 2: 2.
18. Acts 17: 3.
19. 1 Thess 1: 6.
20. 1 Thess 1: 4; 2: 4.
21. 1 Cor 1
22. 2 Cor 1: 8-9.

temperament, this feeling of absolute impotence, of being entirely unable to cope with a situation, must have been particularly excruciating. The same no doubt for the inner torment, the "thorn in the flesh," which afflicted him for so long and from which he sought in vain to be freed.[23] From this kind of situation which makes or breaks, and to which no serious and mature person is immune, there is only one issue—at least for the Christian: "My grace is sufficient for you, for my power is made perfect in weakness." This is in the pattern of him who was crucified in weakness but lives by the power of God.

Of Paul's almost daily consorting with death during the stay in Jerusalem after the three missionary tours we hear at length from Luke, who was with him for part of the time. This writer's habit of describing vividly and at length selected key-scenes in the story, and passing rapidly over the intervals, must not lead us to forget the two years spent in prison at Caesarea, only fleetingly referred to in a subordinate clause.[24] Two years is a long time for a man with Paul's sense of urgency. Then the voyage, shipwreck, contrarieties in Rome and another two years of house arrest, at which point Luke's story ends. If the pastoral letters are from his hand, or even reflect faithfully his condition during the last years, we see that he suffered what Simone Weil described as the only evil—absence, in this case, the absence of friends, a sense of isolation and abandonment: "Demas in love with the present world has deserted me.... Crescens has gone. ...Luke alone is with me."[25] He may well have died almost alone.

Examined from this point of view, therefore, Paul's life is in line with that of Jeremiah, or any of the other prophets, whose mission was accomplished only at the cost of a mounting experience of suffering. But Paul, in the text from which we began, goes beyond what any of the prophets could claim when he asserts that he and all Christians rejoice in their sufferings. The word

23. 2 Cor 12: 7.
24. Acts 24: 27.
25. 2 Tim 4: 10.

which he uses here really means to boast, a point which has to be made in that Paul began in this letter with the purpose of removing any human ground for boasting, since all are under the power of sin.[26] No one can achieve the end of existence, which is to share in the glory of God;[27] this has been made possible only through what God has done in Christ. By entering into a faith-relationship with Christ in his death-to-life act, this possibility can be actualized in a man's life; but it has to be translated into the hard currency of real experience, making the right decisions, endurance issuing in approval or character. This provides the mainspring for a new forward-movement, the direction or sense of which is the Christian hope. This is not just an illusion, since "God's love has been poured out into our hearts through the Holy Spirit which has been given to us." At the same time, hope is not certainty, since the future depends on our decisions in the face of emerging circumstances. We can make the wrong choices, we can sin.

The substantive that Paul uses when he speaks of boasting in his sufferings is *thlipsis,* which means literally "a being crushed," as if by a great weight. This corresponds to what was in effect a technical term in the vocabulary of contemporary Jewish apocalyptic. In these apocalyptic milieux, it was often believed that a period of oppression and suffering would precede the new age of the Messiah. This transitional period would witness at the same time the death throes of the "present age," dominated by evil forces, and the birth pangs of "the age to come." This last metaphor goes back perhaps to Micah, who speaks of Zion as a mother seized by pangs in her labor of giving birth to the Messiah.[28] It is, at any rate, found frequently in the Old Testament and was familiar at the time of Paul. It is explicit in the saying of the Johannine Christ, about the disciples weeping and lamenting while the world rejoices: "When a woman is in travail she has sorrow because her hour is come; but when she is de-

---

26. Rom 3: 9; 3: 19; 2: 27.
27. Rom 5: 2.
28. Mic 4: 9-10.

livered of the child she no longer remembers the anguish for joy that a child is born into the world."[29] The same way of thinking is implicit in what Paul says about their present afflictions to the Christians of Salonika among whom the parousiac hope was particularly strong. They had received the word "in much affliction," but had already been told that this was necessary if the new life was to be born in them. Timothy had been sent specially to remind them "that no one be moved by these afflictions. You yourselves know that this is to be our lot"[30]—understood in the present crucial passage of salvation history. In the second letter their present afflictions are even more explicitly associated with the expectation of the Lord's perhaps imminent parousia.[31] We find a parallel case with the Christians addressed in the Epistle to the Hebrews, who had received the gift of faith amid much suffering, including the loss of their temporal goods, and had to be reminded that this period is transitional and must be endured if the end is to be reached.[32]

Paul's way of coming to terms with his own sufferings was possible only within this eschatological, forward-looking perspective. While this is mostly clearly attached to the purely temporal aspect of the parousia expectation in the earlier correspondence, we can trace, as time went on, a gradual detachment from this limiting point of view. This came about in the first place with the realization of the magnitude of the missionary task he had set himself. The fulfillment of God's plan, involving the bringing together in a new family both those who were near (the Jews) and those who were far (the Gentiles), was still far from complete. But this did not prevent him from seeing the sufferings involved in the apostolate as part of the preparation for the in-breaking kingdom, as God's authenticating mark and the assurance that some day he would show his hand. It is precisely for this reason that he can rejoice or boast of his sufferings, as he does in the well-known autobiographical passage referred to earlier: "What

29. Jn 16: 20-21.
30. 1 Thess 3: 1-6.
31. 2 Thess 1: 5-10.
32. Heb 10: 32-36.

I am saying I say not with the Lord's authority but as a fool, in this boasting confidence. . . . Whatever anyone dares to boast of—I am speaking as a fool—I also dare to boast of. . . . I must boast; there is nothing to be gained by it, but I will go on. . . ."[33]

This rejoicing, even boasting in suffering, is the strange and eccentric element in the Christian attitude. For many it can hardly fail also to be one of the most repellent, and when we remember some forms this attitude has taken in Christian history, there must be some justification for this. An especially clear case is Calvin, for whom *la souffrance est meilleure que la joie;* and the one-sided Calvinist teaching has seeped through into the lives of thousands of people, as widely differing as van Gogh brought up in an avid Calvinist atmosphere, and Pascal, who believed that sickness was the natural state of the Christian. For Paul, on the contrary, the Christian does not just suffer, both in his general humanity and in the particularity of his being a Christian; he rejoices in his sufferings. When we suffer and no longer know why, when we suffer without rejoicing, then we are outside of the genuine Christian experience. That is the simple test. At the same time, this shows up all other explanations of human suffering as insufficient—whether we speak of suffering helping us towards approaching others in sympathy, or building up our own character, or contributing to the building up of the cosmos which, as Teilhard de Chardin has reminded us, involves many failures and casualties; though this last calls for a degree of faith in the cosmic process which, one suspects, only very few are capable of.

In itself, however, rejoicing in one's sufferings might be just another version of the banal injunction to grin and bear it. What Paul shows us through his correspondence, which is the mirror of the high period of his mission, is how this rejoicing is possible. The answer is simply that the Christian suffers in union with Christ. Not just in the sense that Christ, as the supreme artist of living—the phrase is van Gogh's—gives us an example which we are called on to follow; that above all in Gethsemane and on Calvary he showed us how to face "the double agony" of suffering

---

33. 2 Cor 11-12.

and death which is the lot of all of us. This is already of tremendous significance for us today, as it was for Paul's catechu-
mens "before whose eyes Jesus Christ was portrayed as crucified";[34] but Paul goes beyond this. By his baptism, the Christian
is immersed in the redemptive death-to-life of Jesus; he is con-
crucified with him.[35] The sufferings and death of Jesus did not
just happen to him, but formed a positive act accepted in advance and thereby became an event. This acceptance, this event-
character, is expressed by speaking of Christ's obedience—"He
learned obedience through what he suffered."[36] But this loving act
of submission is not simply the archetype of the redemptive
process establishing the Christian pattern of existence—through
death to life. Out of the baptismal faith-relationship of the community with Christ a new and deep level of communication is
created. This implies also a *koinonia* in suffering which both links
together the sufferings of the individual Christian with those of
Christ and binds the sufferings of the whole body together. Paul
therefore can declare that he shares abundantly in Christ's sufferings during his mission, and goes on at once to say:

If we are afflicted it is for your comfort and salvation; and if
we are comforted it is for your comfort, which you experience
when you patiently endure the same sufferings that we suffer.
Our hope for you is unshaken; for we know that as you share
in our sufferings, you will also share in our comfort.[37]

This implies that the Christian suffers not so much with Christ
as in Christ, that he has to appropriate his sufferings in the suffering Christ and thus reproduce on the hard-grain material of concrete existence in this kind of world the pattern of Christ's death.
The key-phrase here comes from Paul, writing in prison to the
Philippians: "... that I may know him and the power of his
resurrection, and may share his sufferings, becoming like him

---

34. Gal 3: 1.
35. Rom 6: 3.
36. Heb 5: 8.
37. 2 Cor 1: 5-7.

in his death, that if possible I may attain to the resurrection from the dead."[38]

This is the constant point of reference for Paul in bearing the crushing burden of the mission. The union between Paul and Christ is so intimate that, when Paul suffers, the sufferings of Christ are renewed as a present reality. This truth, so often presented to us homiletically in a banal way, is in itself so strange that he can express it in its pure state, its native intensity, only by a sort of dislocation of language. He speaks of a con-crucifixion, of carrying about in one's body the dying of Jesus, of making up what is lacking in Christ's sufferings for the Body which is the Church, of the sufferings of Christ overflowing into the Christian. Linked with this is the equally new and strange truth that suffering, the most acute form of which is isolation, can become, if experienced within the new Christ-reality, intercommunicable and interavailable. There is hardly any letter of Paul in which he does not speak of himself sharing in the sufferings of his readers or of them in his. There is therefore no abstract solution to suffering as a problem, only an experience we are invited to share. The experience of the risen Lord is at the root of the Christian mission or apostolate, and the Christian life in general. If this experience is a delusion, then the whole thing falls through and we are left to cope with the pain in our own life in isolation, as well as we can. If, however, Christ is risen, there is this great possibility of which Paul speaks to the Philippians, that we may attain the resurrection from the dead. But if we do, it will only be at the price of sharing in his sufferings, becoming like him in his death.

---

38. Phil 3: 10-11.

Chapter Five

TEILHARD DE CHARDIN ON THE PROBLEM OF SUFFERING

CHRISTOPHER F. MOONEY, S.J.

The effort of Pierre Teilhard de Chardin to assuage modern man's anxiety by elaborating a guarantee of evolution's success is ultimately founded upon the physical relationship between Christ, mankind, and the material world. This relationship Teilhard bases upon the cosmic vision of St. Paul in his letters to the Colossians and Ephesians as well as upon the Church's subsequent theology of the Incarnation[1] and the Eucharist. In this essay I wish to show how Teilhard comes to terms with the mystery of suffering and death in this world of which Christ is physical Center. More concretely, this means establishing a relationship between the evolutionary process and Christ's work of redemption, i.e., His suffering and death on the Cross and His Resurrection in glory. Before we begin, however, an important point should be noted. We are *not* going to deal with Teilhard's approach to the mystery of moral evil in the world. Nor are we going to deal with his

---

1. "The Body of Christ in the Writings of Teilhard de Chardin," **Theological Studies,** 1964, **25,** 576-610.

approach to the death and Resurrection of Christ insofar as they constitute a redemption from sin. This would involve us in a separate area of Teilhard's theological speculation and raise special difficulties not directly connected with the present topic. We shall limit ourselves, therefore, to one aspect of Teilhard's theology of redemption: namely, his approach to physical evil in the world and its meaning in the Christian life by reason of the death and Resurrection of Christ.

Teilhard has a double purpose in treating the mystery of suffering and death. He first wants to remove their scandal insofar as they constitute a purely intellectual problem. He then wants to treat them in their total reality as human problems, especially as human problems in a world that has been redeemed by the blood of Christ. He accomplishes his first purpose by situating the existence of physical evil squarely within his own phenomenological analysis of evolution. "You might think that a world moving toward a greater centration of consciousness should experience nothing but joy. Just the opposite I say. It is precisely a world such as this which ought most naturally and necessarily to experience suffering. Nothing is more blissful than the attainment of union; neither is anything more painful than its pursuit."[2] From an evolutionary perspective, three forms of evil present themselves as a structural part of cosmic development: the evil of growth, the evil of disorder and failure, and the ultimate evil of death. If these three forms are once seen in the context of cosmogenesis, then "this tiny planet of earth on which we are so closely squeezed together no longer looks like a stupid prison where we are likely to die of suffocation."[3]

There is, first of all, the inevitability of pain arising from human growth. All progress in the direction of higher consciousness must express itself in terms of work and effort. Under the veil of security

2. **Esquisse d'un univers personnel** (1936). In **Oeuvres de Pierre Teilhard de Chardin**, Vol. VI. Paris, Seuil, 1955-1965, p. 105. Hereafter cited as **Oeuvres.**
3. **La Transposition "conique" de l'action** (1942). **Oeuvres**, V, p. 119. English trans., **The Future of Man**. New York, Harper, 1964, p. 90.

and apparent harmony that envelopes the advance of man in the noösphere, there is in reality a universe in which the human struggle toward unity is fraught with hardship. For the movement of life is upward, and man, precisely because he can reflect upon this movement, is able to experience both the difficulty of the ascent and the natural inclination to halt. There is indeed a joy in growth that distracts us from the pain, but it is always there. "Arrangement and centration: a doubly conjugated operation which, like the scaling of a mountain or the conquest of the air, can only be effected objectively if it is rigorously paid for—for reasons and at charges which, if only we knew them, would enable us to penetrate the secret of the world around us."[4]

The human mind is not unduly troubled by evil arising from such growth. It immediately tends to rebel, however, when confronted in nature with the evil of disorder and failure. Teilhard wishes to show that this, too, is inevitable, that a world in evolution and a world without disorder are contradictory concepts. If God has chosen that His creation should reach its fulfillment in and through a cosmogenesis, then frustration in all its forms is a necessary consequence. The problem resides not in the Creator, but in the structure of created being. In a bunch of flowers, Teilhard once wrote, it would be surprising to find sickly blossoms, because they have all been picked one by one and assembled with art. On a tree, however, which has to fight the internal hazards of growth and the external hazards of climate and time, broken branches and bruised blossoms are all in the right place. They reflect the difficulty that the trunk has undergone in the process of growth. Similarly, in a universe where every creature formed a self-contained whole, willed for its own sake and theoretically transposable at will, we should find great difficulty in justifying to our intellect the presence of individuals painfully cut short in their possibilities and their upward flight. On the other hand, if the world represents a conquest still under way, if at our birth we are, in fact, thrown into

---

4. **Le Phénomène humain** (1938-1940). **Oeuvres,** I, p. 347. English trans., **The Phenomenon of Man.** New York, Harper, 1959, p. 311.

the thick of a battle, then we can well understand that, for the success of the total effort, pain is inevitable. "Looked upon experimentally at our own level, the world is an immense groping, an immense search, an immense attack; it can only progress at the cost of many failures and much pain. The sufferers, whatever the reason for their suffering, are the reflection of this austere yet noble condition. They do not constitute elements that are useless or diminished. They are simply the parts that pay for the progress and triumph of the whole. They are soldiers who have fallen on the field of honor."[5]

The test of such an intellectual justification of suffering, however, is whether or not it can remove that ultimate scandal to the human mind, the existence of death. Not all the branches of a tree are broken or all the blossoms bruised, but in the end they all must die. "If by chance we escape, to a greater or lesser extent, the critical forms of these assaults from without, which appear deep within us and irresistibly destroy the strength, light, and love by which we live, there still remains that slow, essential deterioration that we cannot escape: old age little by little robs us of ourselves and pushes us on toward the end. . . . In death, as in an ocean, all our slow or swift diminishments flow out and merge."[6] In *The Phenomenon of Man,* Teilhard notes that the radical defect of all forms of belief in progress, as they are expressed in positivist credos, is that they do not definitely eliminate death. What is the use, he asks, of detecting a focus of any sort in the van of evolution if that focus can and must one day disintegrate? Hence the importance of his postulate on the level of reason of a divine personal Omega, whose existence here and now alone is able to guarantee evolution's ultimate success. This supreme personal Center is, in turn, the real object of "man's desire for survival," a desire that, for Teilhard, is the mainspring of all human activity. In his system of thought, man cannot in his heart accept ultimate death.

5. **La Signification et la valeur constructrice de la souffrance** (1933). **Oeuvres,** VI, p. 63.
6. **Le Milieu divin** (1926-1927). **Oeuvres,** IV, pp. 83-84. English trans., **The Divine Milieu.** New York, Harper, 1960, p. 54. Hereafter cited as **M.D.**

Such acceptance would render unintelligible the whole upward universe in which all meaningful progress in the noösphere would necessarily come to a halt.[7]

In an evolutionary process, therefore, in which all persons are destined in and through Omega to reach perfection precisely as persons, death must in some mysterious way contribute to the growth of personality. Teilhard explains this by the specific effect of death upon the operation of radial energy in the noösphere. Readers will recall that for him radial energy is that which tends to draw an element forward toward greater complexity (and therefore greater consciousness), while tangential energy tends simply to link an element to other elements on the same level of organization. True evolutionary progress resides in radial energy, which in man has become psychosocial, urging him forward to ever higher forms of interpersonal communion. In the material world, however, radial energy is not independent, but operates only in virtue of the tangential energies of arrangement and thus under certain conditions of spatial juxtaposition. The significance of human death is precisely the cessation of this dependence of radial upon tangential energy. "By death, in the animal, the radial is reabsorbed into the tangential, while in man it escapes and is liberated from it. So we come to escape from entropy by turning back to Omega: the hominization of death itself."[8]

In Teilhard's system, therefore, the function of death is to act as a metamorphosis between two different stages of personality. Death for man must be considered as one of those "critical points" in evolution, a profound transformation in nature by which something quite new is produced. Man's death shows that radial energy's development must undergo discontinuity at the personal level as at all other levels. Having reached a certain limit of centration, the human person is confronted with a threshold, the "death barrier," before he can enter into the sphere of a Center of a higher order. Death thus becomes a second threshold of

---

7. This basic orientation of Teilhard's thought I have dealt with in "Anxiety and Faith in Teilhard de Chardin," **Thought,** 1964, **39,** 510-530.

8. **Le Phénomène humain,** p. 302. English trans., 271-272.

reflection, comparable in its effect upon the individual to the crossing of that first threshold of reflection, the hominization of the species. Essentially it is not so much a separation of matter and spirit as the occasion for a new relationship between them. "What is waiting for us, then, is the pain of being carried away into the prodigious mass of humanity,—or what is even greater, the pain of escaping, either by a slow or quick bodily decay, from that whole limited framework of experience within which we were born."[9] This understanding of death as a metamorphosis is the reason that Teilhard could write from the trenches of the 1914—18 war: "I feel there is something to be said for a healthy joy in death, for its harmony with life, for the intimate connection (at the same time as separation) between the world of the dead and that of the living, as well as for their mutual union within the same cosmos."[10]

It should be noted again that up to this point Teilhard's purpose has been simply to remove the intellectual scandal of suffering and death. In the context of cosmogenesis, they no longer appear absurd when confronted with God's goodness and power. Yet physical evil is not a mere intellectual problem; it touches the heart of man, causes anguish and despair, and has power to empty life of all hope and joy. "It is one thing rationally to explain the compossibility of God and evil, and quite another thing to bear up under suffering of body and mind."[11] Teilhard is speaking here from experience. "He was indeed an optimist," writes a fellow Jesuit and close friend, "in attributing to the universe a sense of direction in spite of appearances; but in daily life, in what concerned him personally, he was far from being an optimist. He bore with patience, it is true, trials that might have proved too much for the strongest of us, but how often in intimate conversation have I found him depressed and with almost no heart to carry on. . . . He was at times prostrated by fits of weeping and

9. **Esquisse d'un univers personnel. Oeuvres,** VI, pp. 108-109.
10. Letter of November 13, 1916. in **Genèse d'une pensée** (Paris, Grasset, 1961), pp. 186-187. English trans., **The Making of a Mind.** New York, Harper, 1965, p. 145.
11. **Comment je vois,** 1948, p. 19, note 31. An unpublished essay.

appeared to be on the verge of despair. But, supported by his strong will and abandoning himself to Christ, who was greater than all and the whole purpose of his existence, he hid his suffering and took up his work once more, if not in joy at least in the hope that his own personal vocation ought thereby to be fulfilled."[12]

Suffering, therefore, while ceasing to be an intellectual problem, remains for Teilhard the deepest of mysteries. The pages of *The Divine Milieu* are filled with the most poignant lines on the "passivities of diminishment" in human life. There is "the crazy indifference and the heart-breaking dumbness of a natural environment in which the greater part of individual endeavor seems wasted or lost, where the blow and the cry seem stifled on the spot, without awakening any echo." But the internal passivities are more painful yet, and it is these that "form the darkest element and the most despairingly useless years of our life. Some were waiting to pounce on us as soon as we awoke: natural failings, physical defects, intellectual and moral weaknesses, as a result of which the field of our activities, of our enjoyment, of our vision, has been piteously limited since birth. Others were lying in wait for us later on and appeared as suddenly and brutally as an accident, or as stealthily as an illness. . . . Sometimes it is the cells of the body that rebel or become diseased; at other times the very elements of our personality seem to be in conflict or to detach themselves from any sort of order. And then we impotently stand by and watch collapse, rebellion, and inner tyranny, and no friendly influence can come to our help."[13] It is all very well for an intellectual analysis to show that physical evil is inevitable in an evolving universe,

. . . but for our heart to yield without revolt to this hard law of creation, is there not besides a psychological need to find some positive vaue thalt can transfigure this painful waste in the process that shapes us, and eventually make it worth accepting? Unquestionably. And it is here that Christianity plays an irreplaceable role with its astonishing revelation that suffering, pro-

---

12. Leroy, Pierre, S.J., **Pierre Teilhard de Chardin tel que je l'ai connu** (Paris, Plon, 1958), pp. 43-44. English trans., **Letters from a Traveller.** New York, Harper, 1962, pp. 35-36.
13. **M.D.,** p. 137, 83. English trans., p. 92, 53-54.

vided it be rightly accepted, can be transformed into an expression of love and a principle of action. Suffering is still to be treated at first as an adversary and fought against right to the end; yet at the same time we must accept it insofar as it can uproot our egoism and center us more completely on God. Yes, dark and repulsive though it is, suffering has been revealed to us as a supremely active principle for the humanization and divinization of the universe. Here is the ultimate meaning of that prodigious spiritual energy born on the Cross. . . . A growth of spirit arising from a deficiency of matter. A possible Christification of suffering. This is indeed the miracle which has been constantly renewed for the last two thousand years.[14]

The passage quoted above is significant not only because it brings out Teilhard's second purpose in his treatment of physical evil, but also because it makes clear that such a purpose is to be attained only through faith in Christian revelation. "Faith" in this context means "not simply the intellectual adherence to Christian dogma, . . . [but] the practical conviction that the universe, between the hands of the Creator, still continues to be the clay from which He shapes innumerable possibilities according to His will."[15] Consequently Teilhard is about to make simultaneous use of two sources of knowledge, one from human reason, the other from Christian revelation, the data of one leading to a fuller understanding of the data of the other. This method is quite common with him, and what he intends to do here is to use the data concerning Christ's death and resurrection to show with certitude what a rational analysis of evolution could only suggest, namely, that God's plan is indeed to use the deficiency of matter as an occasion for growth in spirit. He is then going to use this conclusion to throw further light upon the positive aspect of Christ's work of redemption and thereby to relate that work more closely to a universe undergoing cosmogenesis. Let us see how he accomplishes this twofold effort.

There is first the certitude that comes from revelation that the true meaning of suffering and death is the passage to new life in and through Christ. "We shall find the Christian faith absolutely

---

14. **L'Energie spirituelle de la souffrance** (1950). **Oeuvres,** VII, pp. 256-257.
15. **M.D.,** pp. 168-169. English trans., pp. 114-115.

explicit in what it claims to be the case and what it bids us do. Christ has conquered death not only by suppressing its evil effects but by reversing its sting. Through the power of the Resurrection nothing any longer kills inevitably, but everything is capable of becoming the blessed touch of the divine hands, the blessed influence of the will of God upon our lives. *Diligentibus Deum omnia convertuntur in bonum.*" This power of Christ to give life shows itself in a special way when, "as a result of His omnipotence impinging on our faith, events which show themselves experimentally in our lives as pure loss become an immediate factor in the union we dream of establishing with Him." Most of all is this the case with that "final stripping by death which accompanies our recasting *in Christo Jesu.*" Just as He submitted to death, so we must "undergo an eclipse, which seems to annihilate us before being reborn in Christ. ... It is Jesus who forewarns us: ... the same pain which kills and putrifies matter is necessary for a person's growth in life and spirit."[16] Let us imagine, says Teilhard, all the anxiety, fear, and pain of the world as an immense ocean. Into this terrible sea Christ plunged Himself and, as it were, absorbed all those waters into His own Body. Through the power of His love, He diverted their whole course. This flood of suffering, with all the treachery of its waves and tides, He vanquished and subjected to Himself.

The great victory of the Creator and Redeemer, in the Christian vision, is to have transformed what is itself a universal power of diminishment and extinction into an essentially life-giving factor. God must in some way or other make room for Himself, hollowing us out and emptying us, if He is finally to penetrate into us. And in order to assimilate us into Him, He must break the molecules of our being so as to re-cast and re-model us. The function of death is to bring about this opening up of our inmost selves which God desires. It will force us to undergo the disunion which He is waiting for. It will put us into the state organically needed if the divine fire is to descend upon us. And in that way its fatal power to decompose and dissolve will be harnessed to the most sublime operations of life. What was by nature empty

---

16. **Ibid.,** pp. 84-85, 112-113. English trans., pp. 54-55, 74; **La Lutte contre la multitude** (1917). In **Ecrits du temps de la guerre,** Paris, Grasset, 1965, p. 130.

ana void, a return to bits and pieces, can, in every human existence, become fullness and unity in God.[17]

This last text from *The Divine Milieu* leads us one step further
in understanding how there can be growth in spirit from a deficiency of matter: through transformation. "It is astonishing that
so few minds should succeed . . . in grasping the notion of transformation. Sometimes the thing transformed seems to them to be
the old thing unchanged; at other times they see in it only the
entirely new. In the first case it is spirit which eludes them; in the
second case it is matter." For the true meaning of transformation
we must look to the Cross. Christ's crucifixion and death "signifies
to our thirst for happiness that the term of creation is not to be
sought in the temporal zones of our visible world, but that the
effort required of our fidelity must be consummated beyond a total
transformation of ourselves and everything around us."[18] The
reason is that "spirit is apparently unable to free itself except
by a rupture, an escape, which is of a *totally different order* from
that slow process by which matter succeeded in elaborating the
human brain." This rupture is accomplished when by death we
transfer to Christ the ultimate center of our existence, and thereby
undergo a radical sacrifice of egoism, "a sort of breaking-up and
recasting of our whole being, the condition for recreation and
integration into the *Pleroma*."[19]

What is continually being lost sight of, however, is that this
growth in spirit is not that of something entirely new. It takes
place precisely in and through a transformation of *matter*. "The
material totality of the world . . . contains a certain quantity of
spiritual power, the progressive sublimation of which *in Christo
Jesu* is, for the Creator, the fundamental operation taking
place." The task of Christ, living in His faithful, is patiently
to sort out from matter these heavenly energies and to unite

17. **M.D.**, pp. 93-94. English trans., p. 61.
18. **Ibid.**, p. 128, note 1, 117. English trans., p. 86, note 1, 78.
19. Letter of January 9, 1917, in **Genèse d'une pensèe**, p. 214.
    English trans., p. 166; letter of December 12, 1919, in **Archives
    de philosophie**, 1961, **24**, 135-136.

them to His own Body. Just as current causes a ship to deviate from its set course, so this influence of Christ, gradually extracting a "chosen" substance, is responsible for "the general 'drift' of matter toward spirit. This movement must have its term. One day the whole divinizable substance of matter will have passed into the souls of men; all the chosen dynamism will have been recovered. . . . Who can fail to perceive the great symbolic gesture of baptism in this general history of matter? Christ immerses Himself in the waters of the Jordan, symbol of the forces of the earth. These He sanctifies. And, in the words of St. Gregory of Nyssa, He emerges streaming with water and elevating along with Himself the whole world."[20]

This emphasis on Christ's power to elevate the "chosen" part of the world will enable us to understand more easily why Teilhard insists so strongly upon a positive meaning for redemption and consequently upon its relation to a universe undergoing cosmogenesis. The French word *élu,* "chosen," is in fact frequently used in the context of a purification of matter under the salvific influence of Christ. "The Incarnation will be complete only when that part of chosen substance contained in every object—spiritualized first in our souls and a second time along with our souls in Jesus—shall have rejoined the final center of its completion." The "attraction or repulsion exercised upon souls by the Cross" is "a sorting of the good seed from the bad, the separation of the good seed from the bad, the separation of the chosen elements." Hence Teilhard's love of the world is not directed to everything created. "The true earth for me is that portion of the universe which is chosen, which is still spread out everywhere, but which is in process of . . . finding in Christ its true measure and substance." The Body of Christ thus appears as "a loving active principle of purification and detachment," and this is especially true of the Eucharistic Body of Christ, as Teilhard points out again and again, for the Eucharist is the presence throughout time of the total mystery of redemption.[21]

---

20. **M.D.,** pp. 127-128. English trans., pp. 85-86.
21. **Ibid.,** pp. 49-50, 115, 96. English trans., pp. 30, 76, 62.

It is perfectly true that the Cross means going beyond the frontiers of the sensible world and even, in a sense, breaking with it completely. The final stages of the ascent to which it calls us compel us to cross a threshold, a critical point, where we lose touch with the zone of sensible realities. . . . But this agonizing breaking away from experimental zones, symbolized by the Cross, is only (and this should be strongly emphasized) the sublimation of that law common to all life. . . . The royal road of the Cross is in fact precisely the road of human endeavor, insofar as this has been supernaturally straightened and extended. . . .

Jesus on the Cross is both the symbol and the reality of the immense labor of the centuries which little by little raises up created spirit to restore it to the depths of the Divine Milieu. He represents and, in a true sense, He is creation, as it re-ascends the slopes of being supported by the hand of God, sometimes clinging to things for support, sometimes tearing itself from them in order to pass beyond them, and always compensating by physical suffering for setbacks caused by its moral failures.[22]

The positive meaning of redemption is, therefore, the support given by Christ's suffering, death, and Resurrection to the whole upward movement of man in the noösphere. Christ gives this support because in Him there was not merely a man but Man, total Man, and hence He achieves in His own Body-Person the purpose of the whole evolutionary process, namely, the spiritual union of humanity with God in and through a purification of matter. For those who are united to Christ through faith, physical evil has once and for all been placed in the service of spiritual growth. "The world is above all a work of creation continued in Christ. . . . Christ saves the world in the sense that without Christ . . . man's effort would be without hope in a final outcome, and this would mean his losing the taste for life and abandoning altogether his task on earth." Consequently Teilhard is against any understanding of redemption that conveys "the impression that the Kingdom of God can only be established in gloom, by thwarting and going against the energies and aspirations of man. . . . The Cross is not something inhuman but superhuman. . . . It has been placed on the crest of the road that leads to the highest peaks of creation. . . .

---

22. **Ibid.,** pp. 118-119. English trans., pp. 78-79.

The Christian's task is not to swoon in its shadow, but to climb in its light."[23]

This "task of the Christian" climbing upward in the light of the Cross is given a final clarification by the positive function that Teilhard assigns to Christian resignation. His concern here is modern man's bitter reproach to the Gospel for fostering passivity in the face of evil, an accusation "infinitely more effective at this moment in preventing the conversion of the world than all the objections drawn from science or philosophy." Christian submission to the will of God is, in fact, the very opposite of capitulation. Far from "weakening and softening the fine steel of the human will, brandished against all the powers of darkness and diminishment," such submission is precisely a resolute resistance to evil in order to reach through faith that "chosen point" where God is to be found. For God is not present simply anywhere at all in our passivities, but solely at that point of equilibrium between our tenacious endeavor to grow and the external opposition that finally overwhelms us. Only at this "chosen point" does our capacity to submit to God's will reach its maximum, for at that moment our submission necessarily coincides with the optimum of our fidelity to the human task. There is thus to be found in Christian resignation a truly human value, a positive aspect corresponding in the individual's life to that positive aspect of Christ's total work of redemption.[24]

As we end this presentation of Teilhard's thought on suffering and death, we are in a better position to understand the relation he wishes to establish between the positive aspect of redemption and his over-all effort to re-think the mystery of Christ in terms of cosmogenesis. Once more, as in his speculation concerning the Body of Christ, there is an interplay of two sources of knowledge. Human reason had led Teilhard to postulate a transcendent personal Center for the evolutionary process, and his Christian faith had then led him to identify this Center with Jesus of Nazareth.

---

23. **Essai d'intégration de l'homme dans l'univers,** 1930, 4th lecture, unpublished, pp. 13, 15; **M.D.,** pp. 116, 119. English trans., pp. 63-66.
24. **M.D.,** pp. 97-98. English trans., pp. 63-66.

This identification, examined in the light of revelation concerning the Incarnation and the Eucharist showed Christ to be Center of the universe in and through the physical omnipresence of His Body-Person. It is this fundamental concept of Christ as physical Center that has now guided Teilhard's whole approach to the mystery of redemption. For if through His Incarnation Christ has become a physical Center for humanity, then His work of salvation must necessarily mean accepting the full weight of that cosmic development of which man is the culmination and principal aim. This weight Jesus bore in His Body, not only during His Passion, but also in the victory of His Resurrection; He bears it now in His glorified Body and will go on doing so until His Parousia at the end of time. Mankind is able to continue its ascent toward personal communion with God only because Christ has broken the "death barrier," and by so doing has transformed physical evil into an instrument for the purification of matter and the growth of spirit. Christ is therefore Redeemer precisely *as* Omega. His work of redemption is, in the present supernatural order, the ultimate reason why there *is* such a thing as evolution in Teilhard's sense of the word.

Projected against a universe where the struggle with evil is the condition **sine qua non** of existence, the Cross assumes new importance and fresh beauty, and is capable of captivating us all the more. Unquestionably Jesus is still He who bears the sins of the world; in its own mysterious way, suffering makes reparation for moral evil. But above all Jesus is He who overcomes structurally, in Himself and in behalf of us all, that resistance to spiritual ascent that is inherent in matter. He is the One who bears the weight that is inevitably part of all created reality. He is both symbol of progress and at the same time its heroic achievement. The full and ultimate meaning of redemption is no longer seen to be reparation alone, but rather further passage and conquest.[25]

---

25 **Christologie et évolution,** 1933, 7-8. An unpublished essay.

Chapter Six

SICKNESS IN A CHRISTIAN ANTHROPOLOGY

FRANÇOIS-H. LEPARGNEUR, O.P.

Anyone beginning a study of suffering or sickness ought to avoid the danger of speaking in a detached, abstract, and academic manner, for we are all involved in this human condition. The person who does not suffer, moreover, is hardly more favored than the one who does. Although these themes refer to sickness, the term "sickness" indicates very simply and briefly the whole existential situation of the sick person, one for whom sickness has become a state.

It is helpful to recall that there do not exist any clear boundaries between the sick and non-sick person except those we determine ourselves. "We live in a state of shaky equilibrium, and the average health of the spirit, as well as that of the body, is a difficult thing to define" (Bergson). Despite obvious thresholds, the physiology of the normal is not essentially different from the pathological physiology. Not only are we all menaced, but more profoundly we all stand in an intermediate state between the fullness of ideal life and death. From this we can see how sickness is an uncovering of the limitations and fragility of our earthly condition. Sickness is a beginning of death. From our conception we move toward death; hence we are all situated between birth in time and death in history. Sickness prepares us to participate at the same time in life and in death. Sickness, a natural phenomenon, participates in the ambiguity of everything natural: in us and outside of us, some forces proceed in the direction of life while others move toward the destruction of life.

It is inexact to say that sickness, understood spiritually, develops man. Like every difficulty and obstacle, sickness is an ordeal which impedes our path. It develops one and diminishes another. It reduces one beneath the normal level of human existence, making him bitter, envious, and aggressive; however, the same sickness for another can increase his mental and moral faculties tenfold. The normal effect of sickness is to preoccupy the subject with himself, running the risk of structuring his vision of the world about his own person and his evil.

Person confers meaning

A sharer in life, the sick person also shares in freedom. By it he can appraise his situation; and even though he cannot change it, he must confer a meaning on it which the brute fact does not have. Since man is never entirely within a situation, a prisoner of it, sickness is then a challenge both to life and liberty. And as pain is one of the forms of consciousness among men, (insofar as suffering strips away masks) it deepens the personality in the proper line of its being, a unique manner of enriching being by plundering it. Pain attacks, so to speak, so that the person defends his own life; in this sense pain is a value. We are indeed always in this perspective of the sick person and at the same time participating in life and looking for a greater participation in it. This fact shows us that the living human being, sick or not, can aspire to a transnatural form of life. He can transcend his situation. This is an essential aspect for a Christian anthropology of sickness.

Life and Death

The dialectic of life and death, constantly met in our natural being by the phenomenon of sickness rivaling with health, is found on a supernatural level in the paschal mystery, lived by each Christian. "If we have died with Christ, we believe that we will also live with him" (Rom 6:8). The word "death" in this context means death to sin, signified and partially realized by a "ritual death" in Baptism; but what is clear is the meaning of suffering which results if this suffering is endured with Christ. We become "heirs of God and fellow heirs with Christ, provided we suffer with him in order that we may be glorified with him" (Rom 8:17). The way of salvation, the unalterable fullness of life, is found mysteriously bound to the way of sorrow taken by Christ during his earthly life. "So we do not lose heart. Though our outer nature is wasting away, our inner nature is being renewed every day. This slight momentary affliction is preparing for us an eternal weight of glory beyond all comparison" (2 Cor 4:16-17). Suffering, sickness, and death assuredly are not the prerogatives of Christians; yet, what is new with Christ and his disciples is the meritorious value which this weakness obtains. In Christ, the dialectic of life and death subsist in a transformed manner; so also for the Christian.

Sickness, in addition to being a participation in life, is also a participation in death. Among doctors and anthropologists as well as among theologians there has been a growth of interest in the human significance of death. If a consideration of death can be useful to understand the general human condition better, *a fortiori* such a consideration ought to be rich for a thorough investigation of the sick person. Death has a double aspect, activity and passivity; and as such, it affects the human being who is both a material substance (a being of nature) and a personal spirit (a transcendent being). When the necessary physiological conditions for life do not exist, we say that the soul leaves the body. This is the aspect of passivity in death, a violent, almost shocking aspect. In this sense, a living being undergoes death as an end, a term, a point beyond which it is no longer capable of going. But, if one considers not only the material, organic pole, but also the spiritual, personal pole, death is also an activity. By death the human person changes his condition yet continues to be; he passes from the condition of wayfarer to a condition of unalterable achievement. Death is the end of one manner of living and the beginning of another; it is resignation for the body but assumption for the person.

Death is ratification

Man differs from animals in that he uses his materiality to personalize himself. Before death, sickness is placed like a privileged moment, a specific phase of this dialectic of matter and spirit. In the measure in which the act of death is consciously assumed by the person, it is the supreme act of the *homo-viator.* The human being realizes himself by it, even at the price of stripping himself of a body. Death is option and judgment, a definitive ratification of our lived system of values. It is above all an act of adhesion to or a refusal of God. Death as activity is not normally a time for conversion; rather it is the final ratification and achievement of a previous journey. The death of Christ is the sacrament *par excellence,* the source of all sacramental effectiveness, the source of all grace. To the extent that we die really and definitively to sin, united to Christ's dying, death becomes for us a sacrament of salvation. The death of the Christian signifies his death to the world of sin so that he can enter into eternal life with God.

Sickness is also a reminder of the precariousness of this life; it is an experience of the diminishment of those biological forces which disappear in death. And so, it is like a forerunner of the process which leads from temporal to eternal life. Sickness ought also to constitute a strong moment in the gradual formation of the self, what Karl Rahner calls the "autogeneration of the person," which is achieved at the moment of death. In sickness we learn to distrust the physical forces as constituting the essential part of our personality. The biological forces indeed make a fine animal, but there is something else in man, something that cannot be mistaken for the natural forces. We sense another force: the freedom of our personality. The irrevocable instant of transition which death represents, affords the self a summit: there, the person is called to decide his life, to give to it a definitive crowning in an act of his deepest freedom. In the measure that the act of death is really assumed as a free action, one can represent death as "an integral act of faith or unbelief" (Rahner). What is decisive in death is not so much that it be the most clear, the most dense moment, but that it provide a key to life. For if the last instant gives to every life its final, total, and lasting meaning, it is because all the preceding instants give meanings to this last moment of human time. In this perspective, even the last sudden change has been prepared for. All of life is present at the time of death, and death is virtually present in all the instants of life. Certainly death is for life and not life for death; but we must admit that the appearances are to the contrary.

Often the miseries of life and the distresses of illness breed such a disgust with existence that death seems a haven where all will soon disappear in eternal rest, in a blessed and absolute nothingness. From this viewpoint there is no preparation for death, since death is simply that which brings rest.

Believer knows revulsion

It also happens that the believer, together with the unbeliever, instinctively recoils before death. Even Christ knew such a revulsion. Nevertheless, a life lived in dependence on God is completed by a Christian death in which all reality is expressed in these several words of the Son: "Father, into thy hands I commend my spirit." Every sufferer finds himself in the situation of the thieves (hanging) near the cross of Christ. He can either hand himself over to Christ, perhaps without knowing too much about what will happen to him, or he can turn his head from Christ to die alone and let his soul fall into nothingness. "When a man dies in the former attitude, freely and with confident faith, renouncing all to gain all . . . man does not die the death of Adam

... but he dies, whether he knows it or not, the death of Christ" (Rahner).

Contemporary existential philosophers have investigated several themes which shed light on the situation of the sick person. The first theme would be that of human contingency; it is ordinarily rather keen in the psychology of the sick. The spirit of a living man is present to the world by his body, by matter. To these things comes the threat of disaggregation which puts an end to personal participation in history. For the sick, contingency no longer appears as a huge academic work, but a stark reality. Another theme concerns the fragility of human nature. If all life is a struggle, the sick person finds himself in the front lines of this struggle, because he experiences it in his own flesh, not in his mind or in his general information about the world. Sickness makes all that is woven around the individual's activity extremely fragile; it is still another invitation not to build on sand. "The sick person reveals to the whole world its state. By his presence alone, he teaches the world what it is. . . . The little ones, the humble, the poor will save the world by the strength of God. This is what the sick remind us of in the Church" (Louis Lochet).

The theme of freedom is another existential dimension for an understanding of sickness. According to this dimension, man is not made but rather makes himself. The more difficult the conditions of freedom, the more necessary is its exercise. How does the spirit react when sickness strikes the body? In reflecting upon the body and its situation, the reaction of the spirit constitutes the personality. We need the body to be free, but we also need spiritual freedom to lead the better part of the body forward in the situation where it finds itself. The "ethic" of a sick person depends on this reaction of personal freedom in a given situation. Every illness is a restriction upon freedom; but in attempting to transcend this obstacle, freedom directs the person along new paths of living. Furthermore, sickness promotes a realistic commitment to a given situation in which the individual has not had a voluntary choice. The sick person realistically assumes his earthly condition with all the burdens which compose this life.

A final existential theme, that of "the other," produces a

paradox; for, while sickness tends to isolate the sufferer, it also makes one more dependent upon others. It immediately affects all of our social relations since it can tend to be a separation from others (because of bitterness, jealousy, and the desire to dominate) or a communion by which one is opened up to others (by allowing compassion and sympathy).

How react to sickness?

Fundamentally, then, how should one react in the face of sickness? Should one adopt a stance of acceptance or refusal? Surprisingly, what is most fruitful is neither refusal nor acceptance pure and simple, but "a synthesis of revolt and acceptance." Man has to accept himself as he is in order to build a better future on the only realistic foundation which is given to him, his present state. But man also has to refuse everything in and outside of himself that limits him unduly, precisely so that tomorrow can be better than today. Without acceptance there cannot be any means to finding interior peace; and without refusal, no progress is possible against the evils of the world. Furthermore, every man put to a test requires the virtue of patience. Patience renders him humble and attentive; it compromises with history. It does not turn the head aside; rather it confronts, even though it fears. Patience is redemptive when it relies on the transcendent: for some, a fatalism; for Christians, the theological virtue of hope. "For me, patience is a thread of which God holds the extremity in his hand, and this certitude makes me happy" (Uebel-Hoffmann).

We cannot overlook the fact that sickness is a severe restriction of human freedom. This is quite obvious on the physical level, and a bit less obvious on the psychic level. The most delicate perspective of the problems touching on the relation of sickness and freedom concerns moral and spiritual freedom, the power by which a man enters freely into the plan of supernatural salvation. Sickness is an (eminent) situation where human freedom is presented with a two-fold option; it can either be an occasion of sin or an occasion for the increase of grace. Like concupiscence,

sickness becomes rooted in the weakness of a freedom which does
not succeed in rendering a person completely master of himself.
This should not astonish anyone, for human liberty is always con-
ditioned in some way. Unfortunately the healthy perceive sickness
in a very inadequate way. If one asks those implicated in sickness,
as doctors, chaplains, or sufferers, the predominant response rejects
the rather frequent attitude of "healthy Christians" who affirm
that sickness and infirmity are ideal factors for spiritual growth.
Very often the healthy propose to us an ideal of spiritual life based
on offering our sufferings, and they assure us that sickness is grace!
Well do I know that everything is grace, but I am firmly convinced that sickness is an evil, an evil which I am undergoing
and which I am seeking to escape from as much as possible. Who
will dare to tell me that this reaction is unwholesome? Certainly,
the effects of sickness, far from making it easier to bring about
a spiritual renewal, complicate the difficulty by weakening the
capacity for seeing higher values by diminishing the person's
interior lucidity.

No meaning in sickness

Sickness delves into the mystery of creation and history. The
Bible requires the believer to refer sickness to God the creator,
to the transcendent God of history who surpasses our intelligence
and the mechanisms which we are able to analyze. Above history,
there is the God who is mystery; and in God, without a doubt,
sickness and death have some meaning. The rejection of evil,
sickness, and death is natural and healthy. In what sense, then,
and to what degree does Christian faith limit it or transform it?
For good reasons, the sick confronted by zealous Christians have
vigorously repulsed a certain mystique of suffering which attributes
a superior quality in itself to what is only a passive endurance
of evil. As a matter of fact, neither effort, nor endurance, nor
suffering, nor time, nor burdens gain any merit—only love; and
love is not a monopoly of one certain category of men. Sickness,
then, does not give meaning to the life of the sick (which is what

they reproach Christians for preaching), but rather the sick person himself gives meaning to the hard, brutal, progressively integrated and assimilated fact of his sickness. There is a certain objective reality to sickness (e.g. bacteria, etc.), but this objective meaning is strictly dependent on the subjective element, that is, a personal subject. Disease is never independent of a person, and so the meaning of sickness arises from a certain relation of evil to the person who is its victim and who stands in need of reacting.

Absolutely considered, sickness has a cause, an etiology, but has no meaning; its meaning comes to it from both a personal and a cosmic historical context. From the personal point of view sickness can be considered as progressive or regressive, positive or negative, according to the meaning conferred on it. Considered cosmically, sickness is a stage of evil in the world in its trajectory toward eschatological harmony, the new earth and new heaven promised at the end of time.

Christ himself has not come to explain human suffering but to dwell in it, to fulfill it and by that to alleviate it, to replace the need for an explanation by his human-divine presence. The Christian meaning of sickness and suffering is to shape ourselves to Christ's suffering. This is not a natural thing, but the fruit of a faith which declares with St. Paul that the power of God dwells in the weakness of human creatures. But this faith only gives meaning to sickness when the subject inserts himself into an objective history of salvation. The vision of faith indicates that suffering builds up the kingdom to come. Without this eschatological realization of the kingdom to come, we would merely be dealing with an outdated romanticism or a too-facile mystique of consolation. The baptized will always have to try to see better what the sacrifice of Christ means for his own life. For some, the sacrifice of Christ is a response; for others, it is a call. In the face of this, we have to learn to make the sorrowful aspects of the world a moment of contemplation. Suffering, which so easily retires within itself, when transfigured can become a sacrament of charity, an effective sign of opening out of one's self to others. Suffering disintegrates the body and its functions up to the very point of our individual personalities and finds in Christ a superior level for the integration of our resources and powers. When we achieve this realization, we will no longer find a paradox in discovering behind suffering a potential for joy—a sentiment in the New Testament which is always found bound to faith and hope in the Spirit.

Chapter Seven

THE LORD OF THE ABSURD: A NON-TEILHARDIAN VIEW

RAYMOND J. NOGAR, O.P.

Reading the Christian account of salvation as an outsider from the standpoint of secular cultural history, it is preposterous from the first page on. That God should single out a handful of disorganized, culturally incompetent, Jewish tribes, mould them into a people, and enter into their history by becoming incarnate, is unbelievable enough. That the incarnate God should suffer, die, rise from death and thereby literally change the meaning of cosmic existence must be looked upon, from outside the Faith, as a fabulous myth. But the question with which I am faced as I reflect on the unfolding of man's existence is: Does the drama of the Incarnation, Death and Resurrection of Christ appear less absurd to the believer? Or, as the writings of Father Teilhard and others suggest, does Jesus Christ present Himself as the God of order, emerging as the ruler of the harmonious, dynamic evolutionary epigenesis? Does He come as the expected one to the scientist, the philosopher, the wise man? Or does He come as an Intruder, the Uninvited Guest upsetting every expectation?

I cannot help but reveal my hand. Each time I return to this question of how Christ presents Himself to the decisive spirit as an inescapable datum, the wedge is driven more deeply between the world of cosmic law and the unforeseen intrusions of God. So crushing was the absurdity of Christ's coming into the world to those who first witnessed that visit, that, from the vantage point of the Cross upon which He met disaster, no man could tolerate His oppressive presence. They all went away. From that time until now, men slowly straggle back to Calvary, and He must repeat the same unbelievable story. Man has found a way to listen to this terrible tale, but he never gets used to it. How any man can find in Christ the Lord of cosmic order is totally beyond me. He has always presented Himself as the Lord of the Absurd.

Christ places himself fully within the revelation of the Old Testament. Not only is he the one whom the prophets predicted; he refuses to abrogate a single moral law given to the chosen people of God. However, he underscores from the outset that the utter hopelessness and despair of humanity is an irreparable moral and religious pathology which successive generations only aggravate. It is not just a natural property of evolutionary unfolding. It is the result of two deeply rooted attributes of human existence: *creatureliness* and *grievous moral fault*. Forgetfulness of creatureliness is the prelude to the fall into idolatry, and the theme of the Old Testament salvation history without which Christ's entry into the world cannot be understood is: God is angry.

Now the anger of God is not to be thought of as a passion for vindictiveness. This is far too anthropomorphic for the reality of religious commitment involved, a sentimentalism into which those people fall who find only fear in the Old Testament and love in the New Testament. Rather, the anger of God represents His intensity of being. "I am who am" is the name of God in the Old Testament, a name so sacred that it was seldom pronounced. This idea of God must not be forgotten if we are to grasp the sense of divine madness of the revelation. The Christian metaphysician is fond of saying that we know more what God is not than what he is. Yet more often than not, Martin Buber has observed, he speaks as though he knew what God is. The Old Testament revelation does not ask a man to make a speculative analysis of the analogy of being; it rather demands of the personal freedom of man that he abdicate everything in the presence of the anger of God, *that he practice creatureliness* in all its bitter humiliation.

A corollary of this spiritual exercise is the readiness of the people for the unexpected intrusions of God into their day, their history. The Old Testament is a collection of records of many centuries of Divine interventions, of *magnalia Dei,* a continual series of prophesies and miracles. These people of God were invited to draw near to God but they were never allowed to forget that He was surrounded by a burning bush. "No one sees God and lives." They were apprenticed in the habit of openness to God. This receptivity, however, was not untouched by terror, anxiety, by the ground of religious perplexity upon which the communion of creature and Creator had to be based. We often hear that God does not ask, nor expect, the impossible. The God of the Old Testament was incessantly asking the impossible. He came into the lives of the Jews in the oddest ways, at the oddest times, making the oddest demands.

In our generosity, we invite friends to come and visit "anytime at all"—just so long as they give us a day's notice. The chosen people were brought up to realize that it is impossible to prepare for the visit of God. Christ was to remind man of the old Jewish proverb: "You know not the day nor the hour. . . ." The prayer of Habakkuk, the Song of the Children, and the Wisdom literatures are filled with the intrusions of God, not only into the life of man, but into the cosmic harmony of the universe. Only little by little did the people of God come to know that the anger of God was a call of love, shaking them from slumber. How often had they cried out that their desolation might be traded for tranquillity. With such harsh contradictions was humanity prepared for what was to be the "hardest saying of all": the Incarnation of God into human history itself.

From the very beginning, Christ mirrored this sign of contradiction in which God's love and His anger are identical. Everything about Christ, when you come right down to it, was intrusive upon a world of order. What He said about His origins, about Himself, what He did, and what He expected of others was strange.

Only His manner was disconcertingly gentle. He drew everyone to Him: children, drunkards, criminals, aristocrats, prostitutes, rulers, professional men, laborers, foreigners and displaced persons. He wept with friends and relaxed with idlers of the tavern. He accused no one, condemned no one—except to keep the records straight among the "religious" about the rights of the angry God. His quiet, friendly, loving, merciful, sympathetic way brought everyone near enough to see what He was about, to hear what He was saying, to receive a personal invitation to follow Him. But here is where the orderly and the gentle ends and the harshly unexpected begins. At once, when He reveals what this invitation entails, you sense the intrusion of the Divine once more.

Who is He and where is He from? You expect Him to say "Bethlehem" or "Nazareth." Instead, He speaks of coming from the Father, where He has dwelt long before there were cities of any kind. He tells of being sent by the Father, whom no one has seen but Him, with a message which no one knows but Him and those to whom He chooses to reveal its contents. He sounds a bit like the angry God Himself with his admonitions to be vigilant, lest God come upon them like a thief in the night. "When you least expect . . ." says this Intruder. He speaks of such familiarity with the Father that either he blasphemes or man's deepest religious understanding has to be revised. There are three Persons in the Godhead, not one: the Father whom they know; the Son who is revealing this hidden truth; and the Holy Spirit who was to come and make plain all that He now spoke in parables. He and the Father and the Spirit are One. What is more, if they wished to be victorious over the crushing misery of human life and inglorious death, they must believe in Him as they do in the Father, follow Him all the way to the death on the Cross. Every word was an intrusion, not only upon their humanity, but even upon their most sacred and hallowed religious traditions. Every word was contrary to their hopes and expectations. Every word was absurd.

Christ's invasion of the life of man went further than His words, which were true to the prophetic form of the *magnalia Dei,* the wonder-working of God. Just as His speech betrayed a disconcerting displacement of meaning to all ideals the Jews held dear, so now what He was doing manifested His intention to upset the cosmos and all its laws. Many men like to see in St. Paul's words that Christ is "the first-born of all creation, in whom and by whom all things exist and hold together" an inclusion of the Redeemer into the very structure of cosmic unfolding. What they fail to recall is that He did not hesitate to shake the cosmic frame to its foundations. Time and space are His, and there is no promise nor hope that the universe will continue to unfold with determined necessity—if it ever did. The scientist can count on the regular motions of the heavens and the philosopher can speculate upon order, but there is not the slightest expectation from the interpretation which Christ has given to His creation that man can rest the meaning of his tomorrow upon his cosmic harmony.

It is not simply that Christ performed miracles. These were just a prelude to the drama which must be placed alongside the events of creation and Incarnation in cosmic proportions and human significance. He voluntarily suffered, died on the Cross, and rose from the tomb, bringing redemption and eternal release to man—a creature entrapped in an intolerable and irremediable physical and moral condition. The absurdity of the evolutionary world of Huxley and the nauseating existence of Sartre touch only upon the creation and its mysterious misery. It is the cosmic act of Divine redemption which has really intruded upon man's existence and has transformed the universe of space and time. It is not only what Christ *said* that challenges our credulity, it is what He *did* that is unbelievable. Who can believe that God so loved man that He would die for him? This seems not only blasphemous; it seems patently absurd.

But it is what Christ *expects* of man which is the crushing blow. In trading the law of fear for the law of love, Christ changed the orientation of man's entire spiritual life. One thing He did not change. He, like the Father, still asks and expects the impossible. He expects a full-grown man, with all the vigor and sincerity of total personal commitment and ultimate decision, to abrogate his precious freedom in favor of entering into the drama of suffering and death—his Life. The man who has not

yet heard this invitation clearly enough, or who is still too dis-
jointed and personally disorganized to draw himself together in
a single act of absolutely free decision, will not comprehend the
terror, the finality, the irrevocable consequences of saying either
"yes" or "no." One day, he will see clearly that no matter how
terrifying are the prospects of decision, he can no longer turn
away.

Perhaps it will come as it did to Peter.

It was one of those grey days, filled with grim skies and the
metallic taste of confusion and bitterness. Christ has just made
another of those statements: "Unless you eat my body and drink
my blood, you shall not have life in you; he who eats my body
and drinks my blood shall never see death." *Credis hoc?* Do you
believe this? Peter must have had that sick feeling in his heart
which Abraham felt as he walked towards Mount Moriah to obey
God's command to kill his son Isaac. There was that old silence
which always accompanied these awful moments. How can a man
be expected to follow *this* man going *this* way? Had not God, the
angry God, commanded him not to follow strange teachings? Had
He not warned against the idolatry, the sacrilege and the blasphemy
of pagan nature worshippers? Eating and drinking this man's
body and blood! Even if there were a mystical meaning which
would remove the vulgarities of cannibalism, it would mean vener-
ating this man as the giver of eternal life—the prerogative of the
One, True God. But what if He is God. . . .

How far we are now from the ludicrous and the laughable,
from the merely mysterious and paradoxical, from the chance
and disorder of an evolutionary universe and from the apparent
meaninglessness of human existence. These are minor absurdities,
and the cries of men like Huxley and Sartre and Camus trapped
in their impossible and intolerable situations, are like those of a
child with a bruise compared to the groans of Peter as he watched
the trusted friends and disciples shake their heads and leave at
this "hard saying." Then he heard the question that struck terror
into his heart, the last one he wanted to hear at this moment.
"Will you also go away?" At the moment least prepared for,
a man suddenly sees clearly the truth of the Divine madness and

can no longer withhold his decision. Peter's answer is not enthusiastic, not generous, but in the face of the absurdity of following this man this way, one has to swallow hard. "To whom shall we go? You have the words of eternal life." Against the dreary sky on that memorable day of another taste of ashes, Peter knew that he was looking into the eyes of the Lord of the Absurd. Half-hearted, slightly bewildered, his reply was good enough for a beginning. Another day was coming when he would have another chance at the question. This time, with his very life itself, he would be able to reply: "Lord, you know all things, you know that I love you."

Part II

THE MYSTERY OF DEATH

Chapter Eight

THE DEATH OF JESUS

LEONARD JOHNSTON

"The only thing I can boast about is the cross of our Lord Jesus
Christ."[1] This is a far cry from the first stunned reaction of the
apostles: "We thought he was to be the one to set Israel free,
but our leaders handed him over to be sentenced to death and
had him crucified."[2] It was not to Jews and pagans only that the
cross was "a scandal, a stupidity."[3] Even after the reality of the
resurrection dawned on them, the cross remained a dark and
painful shadow in the background; the best they could do by way
of human apology was to show that it was unjust, "he was handed
over by sinful men"; and the best they could do by way of theological justification was the assurance that it happened "by divine
foreknowledge," that Christ had to die, according to the scriptures.

The very shame and incomprehensibility of it indeed gives
Paul his first insight into the meaning of this great mystery,
his first formulation of "redemption." Death is indeed a disgrace

---

1. Gal 6: 14.
2. Lk 24: 20-21.
3. 1 Cor 1: 23.

and a defeat; but this shows all the more clearly the triumph and glory of the resurrection. "You put him to death; but God raised him to life."[4] Death is the end; but the resurrection is a new beginning:

> That which is sown is perishable; but what is raised is imperishable; the thing that is sown is contemptible, but what is raised is glorious; the thing that is sown is weak, but what is raised is powerful; when it is sown it embodies the soul, but when it is raised it embodies the spirit—it is a spirit-filled body.[5]

> Christ, having been raised from the dead, will never die again. Death has no power over him any more. When he died, he died once for all, to sin, so his life now is life with God.[6]

This insight is a valuable acquisition in the Church's understanding. For one thing, it makes it possible to see Christ's work as a *transitus* in the line of God's great work in the Old Testament—the exodus, with all the additional insights that flow from this comparison: that the blood of Christ shed on the cross could be compared to the blood of the lamb sprinkled on the doorposts; that the meal in which Christians commemorated Christ's work was a passover meal; that his exodus involved a new covenant, new life, a new community, a new people, new sons of God.

Here is a perfectly valid theology, and one which we hope will never again be lost or overshadowed in our own theological thinking. But valid though it is, we always feel that Paul is never quite satisfied with it. It leaves the death of our Lord in a purely negative role, as simply the jumping-off point for the resurrection: "He died, yes—a pity, a tragedy, really; but don't worry about this; he rose to a new life, and this is all that counts." Yet one cannot really dismiss death like this. Granted that this new life is all-important, did not his very union with our human nature achieve this—"God sent his Son, born of a woman . . . to enable us to be adopted as sons"?[7] And if some further trans-

---

4. Acts 3: 15.
5. 1 Cor 15: 42-44.
6. Rom 6: 9-10.
7. Gal 4: 5.

formation were necessary, could it not have been brought about in some less brutal fashion—simply by a glorious ascension, for example? But between the incarnation and the ascension lies the shadow of the cross. And the death of Jesus, the Christ, the Son of God, cannot be so lightly brushed aside, an uncomfortable incident between two great moments. In human existence, death is more important than this.

Of course Paul was not alone in adopting this view. The early Church was heir to the Old Testament attitude that death—physical dissolution and the extinction of the spirit—was the outward mark of an even more radical disorder in the human state which we call sin. So when our Lord accepted our human condition, he accepted death and accepted also a condition marked by sin: "For our sake God made the sinless one into sin."[8] Death and sin are connected; so that the death of Christ is not simply the unfortunate prelude to the glorious resurrection, but somehow plays a positive part in relation to sin: "He died for our sins and rose to justify us."[9] This found expression in the formula which formed part of Paul's earliest preaching: "I taught you what I had been taught myself, that Christ died for our sins. . . ."[10]

The death of Christ was "for us, for our sins." But this is really a very vague phrase; and different New Testament writers make different attempts to expand and clarify what it implies.

We have already referred to the concept of redemption as a transition from death to life, with the resulting pattern of passover imagery that this suggests, and in particular the idea of the paschal lamb: "Christ our passover has been sacrificed. . . ."[11] Closely associated with this image is the idea of covenant, and the blood used in this ceremonial:

The earlier covenant needed something to be killed in order to take effect; Moses took blood and sprinkled the book and all

---

8. 2 Cor 5: 21.
9. Rom 4: 25.
10. 1 Cor 15: 3.
11. 1 Cor 5: 7.

the people; but Christ has entered the sanctuary taking his own blood; he is the mediator of the new covenant.[12]

On the same night he was betrayed, the Lord Jesus took the cup and said: This cup is the new covenant in my blood.[13]

Almost inevitably this thought broadened out to include the idea of sacrifice in general: "Jesus Christ was appointed by God to sacrifice his life so as to win reconciliation."[14]

Yet this is clearly not the complete or final answer. The further question arises of the efficacy of sacrifices. Our Lord's sacrificial death wins salvation for us: but *how*? Paul occasionally speaks of our Lord's death as "a ransom," as a price he paid for our sins: "You are not your own property; you have been bought and paid for";[15] "You have been bought and paid for; do not become slaves of other men."[16] Paul may indeed be influenced here by the custom of manumission, by which a slave could buy his freedom from his master; but the influence goes little further than the formula itself, and certainly cannot be carried through rigorously to determine the full content of Paul's thought—as if Christ's death were the price demanded by a stern God for the freedom of men in the slavery of sin. Paul is simply trying to express his gratitude for this wonderful gift of freedom, achieved at such cost: "his free gift to us in the beloved, in whom, through his blood, we gain our freedom."[17]

However, the New Testament writers were much more influenced by the picture of the suffering Servant in second Isaiah:

. . . pierced for our faults, crushed for our sins. Harshly dealt with, he bore it humbly, he never opened his mouth, like a lamb that is led to the slaughter-house, like a sheep that is dumb before its shearers. . . . If he offers his life in atonement, he shall have a long life. By his sufferings shall my servant justify many, taking their faults upon himself.[18]

---

12. Heb 9: 18, 19; 12: 15.
13. 1 Cor 11: 24-25.
14. Rom 3: 25.
15. 1 Cor 6: 20.
16. 1 Cor 7: 23.
17. Eph 1: 23; cf. Col 1: 14.
18. Is 53: 5-11.

This was obviously appropriate to the experience of Jesus, and provided his followers with a way of thinking about his tragic death; it was not simply the negative counterpart to the resurrection—it was an act of self-offering, a sacrifice of atonement for sin.

Here is a great theological advance; but it is still not the only way of thinking about our Lord's death. The fourth gospel has yet another way of looking at it. In this gospel, the key to our Lord's person and work may be summed up in the word "revelation." He is the Word of God, fulfillment and completion of all God's words; "no man has ever seen God; the only-begotten of the Father has revealed him to us."[19] Our Lord has come to show God to us—and not merely to show, but to *bring* God to us. The God he shows to us is a God who loves, one whose love expresses itself in giving: "God so loved the world as to give his only-begotten Son."[20] Christ is the full and perfect expression of God's love. Christ, and Christ's words and actions, was not a sort of visual aid enabling us to understand God better; he was God's own gift of himself to us. And that gift was only complete in our Lord's own complete self-giving, in his death. That is why, for John, the crucifixion is not something shameful, but something glorious, a "lifting up"; because if in Christ we see God's glory, his manifestation of himself, then nowhere was it seen more perfectly than in the perfect picture of love on the cross.

Here then we have yet another theology of the cross. Our Lord's death is the starting point of a passover, a transition to a new life. His death is like that of the paschal lamb; it is a sacrifice, a sacrifice of vicarious atonement like that of the suffering Servant; and it is supremely the action of God giving himself in love. So many theologies of the cross—so many *different* theologies of the cross; and though Paul shares something of all of them, none of them are peculiarly his.

His own characteristic way of looking at it follows from his nature and temperament: he is a Jew, a rabbi, a Hebrew of the

19. Jn 1: 18.
20. Jn 3: 16.

Hebrews. Perhaps the most fruitful part of his work was the result of his attempt to bring his Christian life into focus with his Jewish faith—an attempt in which his personal anguish is reflected in the tortuousness of his arguments. These qualities are seen most clearly in his efforts to grapple with the profound truths of human existence as seen by a Jew—sin, death, the law. These three factors are obviously inter-related; but what exactly is their relationship is difficult to say, since they seem to fall into a different pattern with each new train of thought. This is particularly true of the law: the law seems to be responsible for sin. By increasing the number of prohibitions, it increases the opportunities for transgression. It makes conscious and wilful, actions which otherwise would have been covered by good faith. By the very fact of prohibition it stimulates the urge to rebel. And yet the law is something good; it brought wayward men by leading reins to Christ.

Paul's thought is indeed inconsistent, the result of intuitive glimpses of partial truths rather than of a logical synthesis. Perhaps the best attempt to form such a synthesis is that of Père Benoit, which may be summed up briefly as follows.[21]

"Through sin, death has spread through the whole human race."[22] You can say either that death rules men, with sin as the agent of his rule; or that sin rules, with death as the mark of its mastery. It would not be true to Paul's way of thinking to say that this is "only" original sin, an inherited guilt, or "only" physical death. In either case, it is a sad state of alienation from the living God. But it is true that this rule is not complete and total as long as men do not personally embrace it; and it is here that the law comes in. The law puts man face to face with sin in all its clarity, and makes it possible for man to accept it for what it is, and therefore to feel the full weight of death: "Sin used the law to show itself in its true colors and was thus able to exercise all its sinful power."[23] "The sting of death is sin, and sin gets its power from the law."[24]

---

21. **Exegèse et théologie** (Paris, 1961), pp. 9-40.
22. Rom 5: 12.
23. Rom 7: 13.
24. 1 Cor 15: 56.

This is the first function of law; but a second follows from this. It shows up sin for what it is; and, as a proclamation of the divine justice, it calls with austere objectivity for the penalty due to sin: "If you sin, you die." And it is precisely here that Paul situates the death of Christ. His death was an answer to the call of the law. He identified himself with our human, sinful situation: "he came in a body of sin,"[25] "he was made sin for us";[26] he was "born of a woman, born under the law,"[27] and therefore accepted the curse, the ban, the condemnation proclaimed by the law.[28] And so he dies. But in his dying he sides with the law in "condemning sin in the flesh";[29] he fulfills the law's demands completely, so that the law has no more claim on us. "He has overridden the law and cancelled every record of the debt we had to pay; he has done away with it by nailing it to the cross."[30] His death is the end of the law's demand and the end of the tyranny of sin and death.

This, then, is St. Paul's own characteristic approach to the death of Christ. And a very good one too, as far as it goes. Yet one may be excused for not even yet being completely satisfied. In the first place, we may have doubts about the very picturesque way in which it is expressed. Law, Sin, Death, Flesh—all of these are personified and presented as actors in a drama, "entering onto the scene," "ruling," "wielding weapons," "passing judgment" and so on. We would like to probe further the literal value of such figurative language. In the second place, we would like to see more clearly how this view fits with the other views of the redemptive value of the cross to which we have already referred. For although we readily accept that the full reality of God's work in Christ is richer than any single formulation of it, nevertheless it is the same reality that we are dealing with; and

25. Rom 8: 3.
26. 2 Cor 5: 21.
27. Gal 4: 4.
28. Gal 3: 14.
29. Rom 8: 3.
30. Col 2: 14.

we should not expect the various ways of expressing it to be completely disparate.

Let us therefore see if we can reformulate Paul's own thought in more literal terms, and perhaps in terms which may link up with other theologies.

"The law is sacred and just and good."[31] The law is not an arbitrary command designed to secure obedience simply as a sign of our submission. It is the word of God; it is a revelation of God; it is a revelation of God who is himself good and also our best good. It is a revelation of God's character, and of our character as sons of God. It is not simply a veto, still less a juridical enactment of the penalty of non-fulfillment. It is an expression of divine justice, but only in the sense that it expresses the "righteousness" of God; and to live in accordance with this is to share something of God's own being. It is to live as he would have us live, we who are called to be his sons. The aspect of condemnation which is implied in law is simply a negative statement of the same truth: "This do and you shall live; to live otherwise is to die."

The human condition is marked by all the sad consequences of our separation from God—discord amongst men, discord within ourselves, discord with our environment: all that the Bible calls "death." Death is a punishment, not in the sense that it is an act of God's vindictiveness, or even of his justice, but simply as the ultimate assertion of our alienation from the living God. But precisely because that is what it is, it is also a recognition of that absence, a proclamation of our wrongfulness. To use a trivial analogy, if you put your hand in the fire, you feel pain; but that pain is also a statement of the folly of your action. And what our Lord did was to give death that value: sinless, he made his death a statement of the wrongfulness of human life and therefore of the righteousness of God. He made death a *metanoia,* a change of heart, and a change expressed exactly in the terms which marked our having strayed. Sin is a choice of ourselves and a rejection of God. Our Lord chose God by offering himself. It is indeed a demonstration of love, as John has it—a love

31. Rom 7: 12.

patterned on God's own love, expressed in utter self-giving. It is a sacrifice, as the synoptics see it—an offering of himself to replace the choice of self which sin is. And all of this he does through the very mark of sin, which is death. *Stimulus peccati mors!* The sting of sin is death; but Jesus has twisted sin's own weapon out of its grasp and used it against itself. In the very act of conquering, sin is defeated and cheated of its prey. This is the power of God and the wisdom of God. In the face of man's misuse of his freedom, we could imagine various solutions on the part of an all-powerful creator. He might have scrapped the whole scheme and started again. Or he might simply have accepted the situation as it was, and left men to suffer the consequences of their own folly. Or he might have forgiven and forgiven, answering our repeated sins by repeated acts of pardon which released us from the consequences of our falls. But instead of all these, what he has actually done is to accept man's sinfulness, so as to enter into that sinful state and use that very state as the means of returning to him. The bridge between God and man is broken; but our Lord shows us a painful path among the ruins.

Christ does reign from the cross. The glory of the risen Lord is not just the glory of life from death, but life through death, and even in death. John is right: it is on the cross that the transformation of our Lord takes place, from the state of suffering servant of the Lord to the state of son of man in glory: "Father, the hour has come; glorify your Son—give me back the glory that I had with you before the world began."[32] But though John has it most explicitly, the thought is not foreign to Paul. "He emptied himself . . . to death, even the death of the cross: wherefore God has exalted him."[33] This is not merely the reward for sufferings undergone; it is the statement of what those sufferings really imply. It is the astonishing rider to the argument stated by the law: "This do and you shall live; to live otherwise is to die—but that death can become a means of life." Having identified himself fully with our human condition, he did not then discard it,

32. Jn 17: 1-5.
33. Phil 2: 7-9.

but transformed it: "Ascending on high, he captured prisoners."[34] By the cross he overcame the sovereignties and powers and paraded them behind him in triumphal procession."[35] The resurrection and ascension are not just a happy ending to what would otherwise be a tragic story, just as the crucifixion is not just an unfortunate prelude to the real victory of the resurrection. They are the visible demonstration of the reality of the transformation of the human situation achieved in the cross of Christ.

And the Christian life is our insertion into this pattern. The Christian is not one who shares the reality of the risen state in this life. He is one who by the Spirit of Jesus is able to give the same value to his dying life as Jesus did. "When we were baptized, we were baptized in his death; we joined him in death so that as Christ was raised from the dead, we too might live a new life." But that is a life "free from the slavery of sin," a "life for God." Our own resurrection comes later. "We shall imitate him in his resurrection, we shall return to life with him."[36] Meanwhile, we live as Jesus lived: "Always we carry with us in our body the death of Jesus, so that the life of Jesus may be seen in our body," a life of continual self-offering, "consigned to death every day."[37] "You have died, and the life you have is hidden with Christ in God. When Christ is revealed, you too will be revealed in glory with him."[38] Our present life is like that of Jesus, a life of hidden glory, veiled, covered, cloaked by the weakness of our flesh, which is yet also the means by which we express our union with God. "All I want to know is Christ, and the power of his resurrection, so that later I may share his actual resurrection. Meanwhile I share his sufferings by reproducing the pattern of his death—for I am not perfect yet."[39]

We reproduce in our lives the pattern of the death of Jesus. We are baptized in water, which symbolizes both the death of

---

34. Cf. Eph 4: 8-9.
35. Cf. Col 2: 9-15.
36. Rom 6: 3-11.
37. 2 Cor 4: 10-11.
38. Col 3: 3-4.
39. Cf. Phil 3: 10-12.

Christ and the new life which we share: not by a sudden switch of symbolism, but because this very death is, by the self-offering of Christ, a means of expressing a new attitude, a turning to God. We are baptized into this death, and this is not simply an incident, a moment in time, a once-and-for-all acquisition of a new life. It *is* a new life, but it is a new life which is a state, a permanent condition. Baptism is not a magical wand-waving. It is an offer by God, a promise, a guarantee that he will do for us what he did in Christ: to make our dying lives a joyful self-offering. Not so as to remove us from the normal conditions of life, but to make it possible for us to give them a different value; not to transform our situation, but to transform ourselves. Our reception of baptism is on our part a pledge that we will live as Christ lived, that we will go into the waters of death and transform them into the waters of life, that we will empty ourselves and take the form of a servant; because it is in this form that God recognizes us as his sons. The cross in the life of a Christian is not a bitter reminder of our separation from God, to be accepted only with tears or patient stoicism; it is the means by which we, with Christ, express a permanent *metanoia*—an acknowledgment of our separation from God which is also a proclamation of our will to return to him.

The sacraments are the visible application of Christ's redeeming action to an individual Christian in specific circumstances. Baptism applies it to one who newly pledges himself to share the life of the redeemer. The Eucharist applies it to the community of the redeemed who become thereby the body of Christ. The sacrament of penance applies the death and resurrection of our Lord to *sinful* Christians—to those who have pledged themselves to die to the life of sin; who have failed, and here renew their pledge. It is indeed a renewal of our baptism. But it is also a renewal of our pledge *as sinners*—that is to say, not merely as people who have fallen but as people who will undoubtedly fall again; but in whom equally certainly the will to rise again with Christ is here re-affirmed.

Chapter Nine

RECENT DEVELOPMENTS IN THE THEOLOGY OF DEATH

GEORGE J. DYER

Chicago is a curious city, lying as it does on three points of the compass; it has no east side to speak of. To the East lies Lake Michigan, grimly gray or softly blue depending upon its mood. It laps the beaches during the summer and pounds across the Outer Drive in the Fall, proclaiming itself a formidable factor in the life of Chicago's millions. But to most of us it remains a mystery.

Since the sixteenth century death has lain on the eastern point of theology's compass. Like the lake it was an imposing fact but one that occupied little of the scholar's attention. In recent years the picture has changed remarkably, as venturesome theologians have made increasingly frequent sorties into this uncharted region.

Traditionally defined as the "separation of body and soul," death is now seen by some Catholic theologians as "personal self-fulfillment . . . an act that man interiorly performs," as "transformation . . . and final option," as "man's opportunity for posing his first completely personal act." It would be interesting to specu-late on the chemistry that produced this budding theology of death:

the extravagant interest in the subject displayed by the German romantics, the slaughter of two world wars, the personalist and existentialist philosophies that flowered on that bloodied ground, the twentieth-century awareness of the emphatically eschatological perspective of the New Testament. We will have to leave these speculations to some more leisured essayist, however. The theological literature on death is a flourishing forest and what we shall do is to climb the tallest tree and search for a path. The path can be found, I believe, and with a twist or two it leads out on to the broader landscape of contemporary theology. There, as we shall see, the new view of death has brought fresh insight to a variety of topics: purgatory, infant salvation, the redemptive death of Christ, the very nature of the world itself. Our metaphorical tree has three branches: K. Rahner, L. Boros and R. Troisfontaines. Rahner best epitomizes the objections to the classic view of death, while the other two typify ways of doing theology that figure prominently on the contemporary scene.

Analyzing the classic definition of death Karl Rahner concludes that it is important but inadequate. Its importance lies in its underlining the soul's continued existence as well as its new relation to the body. Its inadequacy shows up in several ways. Most important of these is its failure to speak of death as a personal and totally human event. But even as a description of a biological phenomenon it is defective for it says nothing of death's impact on the soul's relation to the world. Nor does it tell us whether the rupture of soul and body is a consequence of the soul's own maturing powers or something that it simply endures.

Death as a Personal Event

Faith teaches us that with death man's state of pilgrimage comes to an end; the fundamental moral decision made by man in his bodily existence is rendered definite and final. In their attempts to specify this doctrine of the faith, Catholic theologians ask an important question. Is the definitive character of death due to the nature of death itself or to God's free decision? Appealing to John Damascene and Thomas Aquinas, Rahner maintains

that the finality of the personal life decision is an intrinsic constit-
uent of death itself as a personal act of man. Death cannot be
merely an irruption from without; it must also be an act that man
personally performs. More precisely still it must be death itself
which is the act and not merely an attitude which man adopts
toward death. In Rahner's view then death is an active consummation brought about by the person himself, a maturing self realization which embodies what man has made of himself during
life. For if man is both spirit and matter, liberty and necessity,
person and nature, his death too must exhibit this ontological dialectic. If death is the end for the whole man, then the soul too
must be affected, not merely by suffering passively this biological
irruption but by achieving its consummation by its own personal
act.

Death as an Event of Nature

As Rahner noted, the classic definition failed to speak of
death's impact on the soul's relation to the world. Does the separation of body and soul imply that the soul is cut off from the
world? A neo-platonic mentality would imply that this is indeed
the case for it equates proximity to God with remoteness from
the world. On the other hand a strictly thomistic metaphysics
reminds us that even after death the soul has a transcendental
relationship with matter, a relationship which springs from the
very essence of the soul. During a man's lifetime his soul must
have some relationship to the whole of which the body is a part—
the unity of the material universe. In death, says Rahner, that
relationship is not ruptured, rendering the soul "a-cosmic" but
rather it is deepened into a "pan-cosmic" relationship with the
universe. This does not imply that the soul is omnipresent to the
universe or that the world somehow becomes the soul's body.
Instead, by surrendering its limited bodily structure the soul becomes open to the universe; it becomes a co-determining factor
in the universe, so far as the latter is the ground of the personal
life of other spiritual-corporeal beings.

In the remainder of his essay Rahner draws on the premises

he has outlined here to investigate the theology of death as the consequence of sin and as a dying with Christ. His subordinate themes are numerous and brilliantly illuminated. Rather than exploring these, however, we shall see how other theologians have approached these basic intuitions.

Ladislaus Boros: A Transcendental Analysis

The German existentialist Martin Heidegger provides Boros (as he did Rahner) with the initial insight in his investigation of death. In his book *Being and Time* Heidegger spoke of death as the fundamental modality of living concrete existence. Any given existence may be understood as an immersion in death, a dedication to death, because it constantly realizes in itself the situation of death. Death is present in every act of existence as its own end, its *perfectio debita,* something not yet possessed yet proper to every being. This Heideggerian insight solved the philosopher's problem of exploring what lay beyond his, or any man's experience—death itself. Once introduced into the structure of our concrete existence, death opens a pathway to philosophy. It can be grasped in the existent being itself at the intersection of the various pointers to death.

The philosophical method that Boros employs is that of transcendental analysis, *i.e.,* an investigation of the acts of consciousness in order to reach the *a priori* realities that undergird them and make them possible. The method is a familiar tool of twentieth century philosophers, men like Husserl, Heidegger, Blondel and Marechal. Among contemporary theologians Rahner, a Marechalian thomist, has employed this philosophical instrument across the entire range of theology with most impressive results. Boros uses it here to probe the mystery of death.

Boros sees a fundamental dualism in man; his existence seems to be hemmed in by the provisional and the temporary, yet at the same time rising into the realms of the final and definitive. By a transcendental analysis of this dualism he hopes to uncover the figure of death lurking in each living existence. To achieve his goal he enlists the aid of a number of modern philosophers:

Blondel, Marechal, Bergson, Marcel. A glance at some of his arguments will show us the drift of his method.

Knowledge, Volition, and Love: Pointers to Death

Following M. Blondel's analysis of volition, Boros finds that in every individual act there is an unconscious *ecstasis* towards God. Human volition always aims at more than man in reality wills in any concrete act. Every time a man wishes to establish his lasting home in one place, the thrust of his being bears him on to fresh spaces. He is really pressing on to a decision in which he may become one with his whole volition. Only in death, however, can he attain a total identity of his original volition and its successive partial realizations. Until then the individual acts of the will are constantly being overtaken by the elemental drive of the will. Thus, Boros concludes, death is the birth of volition.

Marechal, Boros' second ally, noticed that there is also a fundamental dualism in human knowledge. In every act of judgment we relate the whole of being to the individual object of our apprehension by saying that "it is." By saying that a thing "is" our thought stakes out a claim to the whole expanse of being. In other words we strive after being in its whole extent. These two factors in human knowledge are ordained to one another and would conceivably meet in a moment of total self reflection. The way to such reflection, however, is blocked by the material principle in man. So it follows that the first integral act of knowledge, the meeting of the two lines of knowledge in a single act, can be realized only at the moment of death.

The dimension of death is to be found too in the dualism that characterizes human love. According to Gabriel Marcel man is destined to a personal fulfillment which he achieves in a community of persons through love. Love, of course, implies self-surrender, for it means renouncing any desire to manage, to possess the other person. In a great movement of self-emptying the whole of existence must be transformed to the point where everything not directed to the other person must be given up. But here the human heart becomes the scene of a tense drama. For human existence is wrapped up in itself, in a single sinister circle of self-seeking. And here we find the dualism of human love that never reaches the good in itself but only the good that stands in a concrete relation to ourselves. Of course there are fleeting and unstable moments of complete surrender in our lives, but then existence falls back behind the wall of self.

Marcel sees our corporeity as the reason for our inability to stabilize our self-surrender. My body is, so to speak, my absolute possession and all that serves to extend my body establishes with me a relation of possession. Therefore, each act of existence must climb a steep slope if it is to ascend from "having-possessing" to "surrender-being." Through his corporeity man is immersed in the realm of having-possessing and does not own the power to reshape the situation.

At the moment of death, however, the body takes leave of us and the soul is completely exposed. With this exposure, the withering away of all self-centeredness, the soul is at last able to produce something definitive and lasting, something no longer menaced by the provisional nature of having.

Death: A Final Option

Boros completes his demonstration by an analysis of the dualism in existence itself, in the poetic and kenotic (self-emptying) experiences. The analysis, he feels, shows that man throughout his life has anticipated death as a fully personal act. He would, therefore, revise the traditional definition of death by a final consideration of the destruction of the soul. The soul does disappear in the sense of undergoing an "annihilation," a violent removal from the body and its worldliness; moreover, it goes down to the roots of the world and acquires a cosmic relation to existence, a total presence to the world (and here he is indebted to Rahner's view of the pan-cosmic nature of the separated soul). Relating these considerations to his earlier analysis he sees death as a total self-encounter and at the same time as a total presence to the world. In the very moment when it is possible for man to realize the dynamism of his essential being he is transported to the

place where the whole of creation awaits God. Here he encounters
the Lord of the world and makes his final decision, a decision
that lasts for all eternity for the simple reason that it is not made
in the midst of the dualism that marks our present existence.
Act becomes being, decision becomes state, and time becomes
eternity.

Boros' new picture of death finally emerges: "Death is man's
first completely personal act, and is, therefore, by reason of its
very being, the place above all others for the awakening of consciousness, for freedom, for the encounter with God, for the final
decision about eternal destiny."

Troisfontaines: *Death and the Law of Human Growth*

Roger Troisfontaines is perhaps the most distinguished disciple
of the personalist philosopher Gabriel Marcel. In an earlier book
he used the theme of personal growth to synthesize Marcel's
philosophy; here he again employs the scheme in order to illuminate the mystery of death. Troisfontaines sees death not as a
problem but as a mystery. A problem is susceptible of that complete objectification of which science is the master. A mystery,
on the other hand, is a riddle in which I am so caught up
that its solution lies only along the line of personal involvement.

Involvement, or *participation,* are important words if we are
to understand the structure that the author builds around and
into death. For they epitomize the law of personal growth, and
death is a pivotal moment in the growth process. If we are to
understand this connection between death and personal growth
we must follow Troisfontaines as he traces the path of the latter.
As we shall see, personal growth is the passage from the level of
existence (community) to the level of being (communion).

The unborn child obviously is given an existence he did not
request, a heritage and environment he could not choose. He did
not select his parents or his race, or the time and place of his
birth. He is borne along on the pre-existing currents of family
and society. Soon, however, the conscious self awakens and he
rises high enough above the currents to accept or to fight their

obscure forces. Born into a community whose structure was imposed upon him, he gradually becomes aware of his personal
autonomy. His actions become increasingly independent; the environment that once held him widens; self-consciousness deepens;
he realizes more and more his capacity for determining the type
of relationship he wants to maintain with his given situation. This
process of determination is what Troisfontaines means by involvement, or participation.

Man must live in participation if he is to grow. He has been
thrown into existence by a combination of relationships in which
he does not participate even as a subject. To expand fully his
personal being he must consciously and freely assume another set
of relationships. His personal growth then is a passage from the
level of existence to that of being, and the point of passage is
his choice for communion with God and man in faith and love.
Failure to choose communion, therefore, is a refusal to grow.
This law of growth can be observed all through human life, in
adolescence, young manhood, maturity. At first blush, however,
it would seem to lose its validity in old age. Nonetheless, the
law is still valid and it leads us into the mystery of death.

Death: *A Passage to Being*

In old age activity dwindles, the environment narrows, consciousness and freedom seem to diminish. The weakening body
can no longer supply adequately the energy needed for the psychic
and spiritual life. Formerly a necessary condition of subjective
activity, the body has now become a hindrance. Nevertheless,
similar situations found in earlier periods of human development
suggest that the law of growth is still at work. The womb which
was an absolute condition for life during the pre-natal period
becomes an obstacle the moment that the human being is about
to be born. The same thing happens to later substitutes for the
womb, like the mother's lap, home, family, school. The human
being grows by tearing himself away from previous environments
which have become like so many prisons.

In old age the person is preparing to leave an environment

no longer capable of supporting his growth. The passage takes place in death; here the body, a provisional womb so to speak, is abandoned so that personal growth may go on. The entire process of human personal growth, moreover, suggests that within the very phenomenon of death there is activity. In this hypothesis the human person, more conscious and free than ever, turns towards a limitless horizon. In elaborating this hypothesis of activity in death Troisfontaines recalls the phenomenology of human growth: growing activity, widening environment, deepening consciousness and liberation.

As the human being progresses from conception to maturity the activity-passivity balance tips more heavily toward the activity side. Full activity, however, is beyond man so long as he lives. He is limited by the raw material of his body and its environmental extension. Full activity, therefore, would seem to be possible only on a departure from the body. And since the body is the center and symbol of every personal relationship, departure from the body will mean that every relationship, every value, will be questioned again in a most radical manner. Once again the human person will have to take a deliberate stand regarding the universe, God, his fellows, and himself.

Death: A Final Decision

Only in death does man come to a total intuition of himself. For while the body is a condition of earthly existence it is also responsible for darkening the mind. As the infant must leave the womb to carry out its own biological functions, so also the soul must leave the body if it is to carry out fully its own proper activities. Grasping his own self to the very depths man will then discover the full dimensions of his relationships to himself and the world, preparing him for that one perfect act of freedom on which all depends.

While on earth man can only mark the direction of his freedom. He is becoming free but he is not yet free in the full sense of the word. Every choice offered his precarious and developing freedom is only a rehearsal for a future final option. The life of the embryo is a preparation for the life after birth; so also this life is a preparation for that found in death and there is hardly any common measure between the two states. Life on earth represents in relation to our being what prenatal life represented in relation to our becoming. If life is an "apprenticeship for death" then the all important act of our earthly life is its very last act, the act of death whereby becoming yields its place to being.

At the moment of death then man is freed of his subjection to the world of determinism and restraint. He sees in their full reality God, the world, and his fellow man. What he does then is to constitute that reality for himself—his being with them or without them. In a consummate, irrevocable act of freedom he chooses communion or isolation, friendship or hatred. And his being (as distinguished from his existence) will be determined precisely by the stand he takes. Since the choice is made in perfect consciousness, there is no need for him to restate the question. His decision is beyond recall.

Theological Reflections: Universal Redemption

As Boros points out, a philosophical hypothesis is of value to the Catholic theologian to the extent that it demonstrates the homogeneity of a theological truth or shows the interrelation of a number of these truths. When it does this, it suggests that the hypothesis itself is valid. Boros, like Rahner and Troisfontaines, shows the impact that their view of death can have all across the theological spectrum.

The "salvation of the unbeliever" is a classic question in theology, and over the years theologians have given it various answers, appealing to a special revelation, baptism of desire, even an unconscious *votum* of baptism. More recently we have read of the "hidden encounter with God" and the "anonymous Christian." When death is viewed as a final option, however, the old problem is placed in a new perspective. For at death each

man encounters Christ personally and with the total power of
his being chooses either to reject Christ or to establish a personal
and definitive relationship with him.

The ancient question of infant salvation also finds a new
solution. A considerable literature in recent years has expressed
dissatisfaction with the notion of limbo and sought a way to
salvation for the child dying without baptism. In the hypothesis
of death as a final option the infant would have the opportunity
for a fully mature decision at the instant of death. While countless
children may leave us in infancy, therefore, no one dies an infant.

Purgatory

Two considerations must be present in any acceptable view
of purgatory: the removal of venial sin and satisfaction for the
temporal punishment due to sin. The first has always puzzled
theologians for they wondered how a man, past death and merit,
could have his venial sins forgiven. When death is seen as perfect
self-fulfillment, however, the problem vanishes. In death, the
final act of our state of pilgrimage, the just soul's strength flares
up in charity, meeting God in loving devotion and wiping away
all venial sin. The satisfaction for the temporal punishment due
to sin may also be seen in a new light. For the process of purification assumes the dimensions of an encounter. The basic decision
for God made in death penetrates all the levels of our human
reality, carrying along with it all that impedes or slows it down.
These layers of reality are the modes of our existence built up
in the course of our historical development. As the pure love
of God burst forth these modes of being are swept away wherever they impede our movement toward God. In a sense our
whole existence is broken up, a truly painful experience that
could be a means of satisfaction. Seen in this way purgatory
would be an instantaneous thing, the very passage which we
effect in our final decision.

Christ's Redemptive Death

We were justified by Christ's obedience "unto death." But why is there this insistence on the importance of Christ's death? Why could not any moral act have been the adequate expression of Christ's redeeming obedience? In the hypothesis of death as a fulfillment, a possible answer emerges. The developing human reality of Christ reaches its perfection in death; it was only at this moment that he was able to give the fullest human expression to his redemptive obedience.

The new view of death also offers an explanation for the long-recognized instrumentality of Christ's body in the work of our redemption. For by death man enters into a real ontological relation with the universe; he does not simply withdraw from matter but rather enters into a closer proximity with matter, into a relation with the world extended to cosmic dimensions. The metaphysical place where total presence to the world occurs may be described imaginatively as the "heart of the universe, the root of the world." In the hypothesis of a final decision death is seen as a descent into the unity at the root of the world. Thus Christ's soul in death "descended into hell," to the heart of the cosmos where it entered into an open ontological relationship with the universe. The cosmos in its totality became the instrument of Christ's humanity, the instrumental cause of grace for every man. When Christ's human reality was planted in death at the root of the world, it grounded a scheme of salvation which embraced the entire human race.

At the moment when Christ descended into hell the world was transfigured and became a vehicle for man's sanctification. This transformation is a present reality, awaiting only the parousia for the final revelation of what has already happened in the depths of the world's being. This view of the descent into hell corresponds with Paul's allusion to Christ's disarming the principalities and powers. These intermediary forces (exegetes differ in seeing them as good, evil, or indifferent) had their place in the structure of the world as powers in the cosmos. Christ did away with them and himself became the inmost center of history. And from this divinized core of the universe new forces are already flowing into our existential environment. This idea, of course, is reminiscent of the intuition of Teilhard de Chardin. In his world view Christ is everywhere present in evolution as the most intimate of all the energies at work in the process. Thus the universe is, in Teilhard's phrase, a "divine milieu."

Resurrection and Ascension

The ultimate finality of a world permeated and transformed by the spirit has already dawned although it is still hidden, awaiting its manifestation at the end of time. The sign that this working of the spirit has already taken place is Christ's risen body. His body, no longer subject to conditions of time and space, permeated by the spirit, is the archetype of a universe that has already been transfigured. Free of all the restraints imposed by spatial and temporal dimensions, Christ is able to reach men of every time and place and to make them members of his transfigured body.

The ascension is the immediate consequence of the resurrection, coinciding with it in time and essence, for it is the entrance into the sphere of God's glory. Luke presents a problem for this view, of course, when he speaks of the forty days intervening between resurrection and ascension. The difficulty can be resolved by seeing two aspects of the ascension: the exaltation of Christ to the Father and the visible manifestation of this departure from the Mount of Olives. Seen in this way the ascension of which Luke speaks is a sign that the period of intimate association with Christ is over and that he will come no more until the parousia.

Conclusion

If we have dwelt perhaps overlong on the methodologies of these theologians it is because they typify several approaches to what may well be the central problem of contemporary theology —the problem of meaning. If theology is not to retreat to the cloister or to the university, it must learn to speak to contemporary man in a language that is meaningful to him. Much of our traditional religious language, including such terms as "sin, guilt, grace, justification," have lost their significance for a host of our contemporaries. A simple explanation of the terms will not suffice to remedy the loss; somehow the content of our theology must be related to the substance of contemporary experience. Each of the theologians of death has responded to this challenge in his own way. With what success they have done so I leave the reader to judge. None of them, however, has escaped criticism.

There are obvious limitations, for instance, to personalism as a theological tool, and Troisfontaines is aware of them. If personalism probes dimensions of reality that are difficult to capture in the categories of scholastic metaphysics, it also reaches a boundary beyond which it cannot move. It can suggest the survival of the human person after death, but it can do no more than this; here Troisfontaines falls back upon the more traditional metaphysics. He faces a more serious objection than this, however. For it is indeed anomalous to hear a personalist saying that the soul apart from the body is in a better position to be a person.

Some of the more fundamental intuitions of these theologians, fascinating as they are, have also drawn the criticism of their colleagues. Not all like Rahner's generalization of the notion of matter in his account of the soul-body union; for it would seem to dissolve the only means of establishing the personal identity of the separated soul. Rahner and Boros have been criticized too for assigning the death of Christ too positive a function in the redemptive process apart from the resurrection. In neither New Testament view of the relation of Christ's death to his resurrection (that of Paul and John) could it be said that a new positive relationship to the world was established by the fact of death itself. And Christ, it is further suggested, did not reach the root of the world by his descent into hell but rather by his exaltation at the right hand of his Father.

There also seems to be a bit of theological sleight-of-hand in Boros' solution to the problem of the baptized infant's final option. "*In sensu diviso* even infants who die in their baptismal grace can make their decision for God or against him; *in sensu com-*

posito (*cum gratia baptismatis*) their decision, in actual fact, is made for God."[1]

In recording these criticisms I wished only to bring the contemporary picture of death somewhat into focus. For these theologians not only expect but hope for the judgment of their colleagues, knowing that only in the collision of ideas can theology hope to progress.

---

1. Boros, L., **The Mystery of Death,** New York: Herder & Herder, 1965, p. 185, n. 54.

Chapter Ten

DEATH AS ACT:
AN INTERPRETATION OF KARL RAHNER

ROBERT J. OCHS, S.J.

That death is a passive, natural event is evident enough, and
our remarks on this heading were accordingly limited to showing
that one must not overlook this aspect of death. But that death
is a personal act is a less familiar idea and will require more
explicit treatment. It is an idea of considerable importance in
the theology of death, since the whole analysis of death as a
tension, as ambiguous, and as the locus of faith and hope, depends
on it. If death is merely passive, merely something that happens
to us but does not concern us personally, something toward which
we need take no particular attitude, then it poses no existential
question to man at all, and is religiously indifferent. What then
is meant by death as act, as a personal event?

First, what is *not* meant? Death as a personal event in **Rahner's**
technical sense is not to be confused with the personal style
a few heroes manage to give to their deaths, so that in their
deaths they sum up their lives in some gesture which finishes
off the whole like a melody. A few people take their leave this

way, but for most men life is interrupted before the measure is over.

Death as a personal event does not mean a person is lucid or illuminated at the moment of death. It does not imply that man will be given a final chance to opt for or against God at the end of his life. It does not mean to valorize man's last moments above the rest of his life, to give added significance to deathbed conversions or lapses, often made when a person is hardly himself. Such a conception of the moment of death cheapens the rest of life, reducing it to a kind of rehearsal. It takes the existential pressure off the present moment, where the real decisions have to be made. It would tend to imply that the decisive moment will always come later, that the present moment, at any rate, is not it.

The traditional discussion about perseverance and presumption need not be interpreted, therefore, in terms of death as the decisive moment. That nobody this side of death can consider himself confirmed in grace or hopelessly lost in sin is a statement about man's present attitude, that it is never to be regarded as fixed and accomplished, secure beyond temptation or impervious to repentance. Its effect is to give to the present its full existential weight, by considering the past as flexible and not as fixed. It dislodges a man, prevents him from settling down and regarding his life as basically accomplished. It seeks to describe man as *homo viator,* man the wayfarer. It would be to go to the opposite extreme to turn this meaning upside down and consider death as a guaranteed further chance, the last chance. Instead of focusing attention on that future into which the present opens, it would distract attention from it in favor of some distant future.

That death is personal fulfillment does not mean either that life goes on maturing despite the appearance of decline, senility and so on, as if people necessarily became wiser or more serene with age. Experience shows too well that aging has a way of loosening a man's grip even on his own wisdom. All a person has painfully built up in the way of wisdom can be dismantled by age. We are not looking, then, for some area in which man does go on maturing, some area such as wisdom or serenity.

What does Rahner mean by it then? Why is death a personal act? How to approach this key insight?

Two Approaches

He makes a double approach, and thus seems to mean two distinct but related things by personal death. One approach is from death as the end of the time of pilgrimage, death as somehow intrinsically connected with judgment. This approach, developed in the early pages of his article, "On the Theology of Death," might be called the theological approach arguing downwards from above, from death as judgment, death as fixing one's life-decision for eternity. Even so, there are phenomenological elements to this approach, elements of an approach from below, for instance in the exigency for definitiveness that dwells in all moral decision.

The second approach might be called an existential one. It is the one Rahner uses to develop the "voluntary" nature of death in his essay on martyrdom. Its point of departure is that man is a person with "an imposed liberty," which he must make into "a free liberty."[1] Man must assume his de facto self freely, take it up with all that it implies. He must affirm his death. How these two are related, how the exigency for fulfillment fits in with one's effort to affirm the event which seems to deny this fulfillment, will occupy us after we have described each of these approaches in detail.

First Approach

The approach from death as the end of man's state of pilgrimage proceeds from man, not so much as nature, but as person. Nonetheless, this aspect is admittedly a formal, not existential one. According to this approach, death brings to man, as a moral and spiritual person, a finality and a consummation which renders

---

1. Karl Rahner, **On the Theology of Death,** New York: Herder & Herder, 1965, p. 86.

his life-decision for or against God final and unalterable. This does not preclude further development after death. In fact, it is impossible to conceive the eternal life of the transfigured spirit in the immediate company of the infinite God otherwise than as a never-ending movement of the finite spirit into the life of God. But the affirmation of faith concerning the definitive ending by death of the state of pilgrimage means "that the fundamental moral decision made by man in the mundane temporality of his bodily existence, is rendered definite and final by death."[2] Such a doctrine takes this life with radical seriousness. Life is truly historical, that is, unique, unrepeatable, of inalienable and irrevocable significance. Life is suspended between a genuine beginning and a genuine end.

"The end of man as a spiritual person is an active consummation from within, a bringing of himself to completion, a growth that preserves the issue of his life; it is total entry into possession of himself, the state of having 'produced' himself, the fullness of the being he has become by all his free acts."[3] This idea may seem less strange when it is pointed out again that Rahner does not mean all this of the precise clocktime moment of death. The moment of death does not provide a special illumination; the aspect of death as act and completion does not cancel out the opposing aspect of death as suffering and powerlessness. But Rahner does mean that man's fundamental moral option, which has been maturing during his lifetime, eventually becomes definitive, and that this end is somehow connected with death.

This view is ultimately imposed by the dogmatic propositions gathered under the rubric of death as the end of the time of pilgrimage. There is no second chance, no transmigration of souls, no general apokatastasis or general restoration. This life we know is taken quite seriously for the historical thing it is, i.e., it is unique, unrepeatable, irrevocable, going from a real beginning to a real end. Rahner insists that this finality is an inner factor

---

2. **Ibid.,** p. 27.
3. Karl Rahner and Herbert Vorgrimler, **Theological Dictionary,** New York: Herder & Herder, 1965, p. 117.

in death itself, not just something arbitrarily connected with it by God. God makes man's death to be his judgment, because man has himself reached his definitive state in and through death. Final damnation is definitive, because man himself has made it final, precisely in the act of death.

To link the finality of the personal life-decision only arbitrarily with death obliges one to look for other reasons for the perseverance of the saved and the damned in their decisions. But looking for such reasons betrays that one is thinking, in spite of oneself, of eternity as just an extension of time, where we ride on as before, except that we shall ride on new horses (according to the image of Feuerbach which Rahner is fond of citing, and which is a very revealing example). To imagine the possibility that a decision could be changed in eternity shows that one is thinking of time and of human decision quite apart from one another—as if time and eternity were just two different periods in which we could do our deciding, or two different horses on which we might ride.

Rahner, however, conceives time and eternity strictly in terms of freedom. "Time is primarily the mode of becoming of finite freedom."[4] Eternity is the product of time. What comes to be *in* time, as its own matured fruit, is *eternity,* which does not so much continue time after it has been lived out, as it puts an end to time, in that it is released from *that* time which lasted for a while just so that something definitive could be worked out in freedom.[5] If the personal life-decision becomes definitive in death because of what death is, and not because of some arbitrary decree, then death must not be just a free act, but a special kind of free act, *the* free act, final and definitive by its very nature. Instead of being a decision that for some reason can't be taken back, it is a decision that won't be taken back.

An act that has such a hold on itself is not easy for us to imagine, because we have no direct experience of such an act. It is only present in our experience as a dynamism, an ideal,

4. **Ibid.,** p. 461.
5. Karl Rahner, **Theological Investigations,** Vol. IV, Baltimore: Helicon Press, Inc., 1961-67, p. 348; Rahner and Vorgrimler, **Op. Cit.,** p. 151.

a desire which is implicit in our important choices and which makes them possible. But despite our desire to commit ourselves completely and for good, all the free commitments we make during life are reversible. We can regret them, fail to live up to them, betray them, no matter how definitive we had meant them to be. This is to say that they are all made in time, that they do not give birth to eternity.

This is also true of our basic commitment for or against God, our basic option. We are never so much the master of ourselves that we cannot go back on it. In this sense, it is an immature, unripe decision all our life long. But it is ripening all the while, until at the end of our lives it has reached its maturity. Then it becomes final, because it will not be changed. At that point, it is no longer temporal, but eternal.

The final act, then, by which we are judged for all eternity, is not just the last act of a series, which, for some mysterious reason, God chooses to weigh more heavily than its predecessors, but an act which sums up all the others, the résumé of a lifetime, the authentic expression of ourselves. We need not fear being judged for an act done when we were not at our best, or not our true selves. The act by which our eternal destiny is decided is supremely representative of what we really are. Judgment is not a balancing off of good deeds against bad. There is ultimately only one deed, good or bad, of which our good and bad deeds are more or less completely integrated elements.

To speak of death in this way is to affirm that at bottom life is a unit, a whole. Or rather, it is to affirm, against so many appearances to the contrary, our ultimate power to give it a unity. Our final act of integrity is precisely an act of integration, by which we finally manage to give a consistent meaning to our lives, so that it all makes sense and makes *one* sense. Each free act involves an interpretation of oneself and one's life, and death is the final interpretation we give our whole life.

Thus Rahner, in insisting on death as a fulfillment, is trying to do justice to two truths. Firstly, we live out *one* lifetime, and yet, secondly, this one lifetime is a life*time*. It is a unity and yet it develops through stages. It is a span between a true beginning and a true end.

These notions of "beginning" and "end" apply strictly only to the "spiritual-and-personal," the *geistig-personal,* the only beings who have a history properly so-called. For a spiritual-personal being, the end means the free and active acceptance of its true beginning. But not until we understand end as the end of a history lived out in freedom before God, do we have the properly theological notion of end, and with it, the theological notion of death. End does not, therefore, represent an arbitrary caesura in time, but a true fulfillment of time.

Thus the argument proceeds from a complex of theological truths revolving around judgment: we are judged for what we are, on the basis of the whole of our life, when we are at our best. Judgment is the unveiling of what we really are, our basic option, which lies inaccessible beneath a veil of ambiguity all our lives. This judgment is irreversible; its outcome is decided in this life, is, in fact, the decision of this life. It therefore is intimately connected with death, which concludes this life.

This is judgment put passively. The whole complex put actively means that the Christian person adheres to God actively, wholeheartedly, with all he is. It is the fulfillment of the command to love the Lord with one's whole heart and mind and strength. Man is a free, adult partner in loving God. This implies that his life must make him capable of this. If God is just a reward for good behavior, but is not chosen for who he is, however implicitly, during life, man never possesses God freely. Either man chooses God wholeheartedly in his lifetime, or he never does. Otherwise, judgment would mean counting a less than wholehearted act for the whole, and giving man the whole in the beyond on the merits of a partial act during life. Such a conception goes against the very idea of freedom. If a man were first capable of wholehearted acceptance of God after death, he would in fact be first choosing God after death. This would devalue temporal life utterly, or at least make it no longer the only time of pilgrimage. The decision for or against God would take place in the beyond.

Why then, ultimately, must death be this kind of personal act? Basic to Rahner's whole conviction is the idea that death is something which affects the whole man, soul and body, i.e., soul as well as body. The dominant Neoplatonic orientation of eschatology since the first days of theology, against which both Catholic and Protestant theologians, in their different manners, have passionately reacted in recent years, often came near saying that the soul did not die at all, but only the body. It is jarring to note that the unfortunate expression "immortality of the soul," if taken literally, says this very thing. Of course, most theologians who have been content to use the expression have merely meant by it that the soul does not become extinct at death. But a dualistic anthropology will almost inevitably conceive this survival, this "immortality," as a living on of the soul after death, i.e., after that particular event which means for it the loss of its body. The overcoming of this dualistic anthropology in recent philosophy has caused renewed interest in death as an event affecting the soul, the person. To say that death is an event of the soul is to say more than that the soul merely continues to exist, or that it merely experiences the loss of the body. The death experience must be an experience in the order of soul, or better, of person, and therefore of freedom, self-realization. That is why death must be an act "from inside," with all that this implies.

Thus if death is an event of the whole man, there must be a legitimate "reading" of it as an event of the soul and not just of the body, as a "personal" as well as a "natural" event. But to read death as personal is nothing other than to read it as an act of freedom which sums up a person's life once and for all. Freedom means, precisely, disposing over oneself in a way that is constantly reaching for the ultimate, definitive, degree. Freedom is not the capacity to realize this or that thing, but to realize oneself once and for all. Rahner's reading of death as act is then the application of this understanding of human freedom. Or rather, it is a consequence of it, a meditation on freedom's urge to realize itself once and for all. This "once and for all" present in all acts of radical freedom as an ideal, a horizon, is death itself, the *once* which gathers up the moments of a lifetime and asserts them once and *for all,* for eternity. In this one phrase is gathered the whole complex: freedom-time-eternity.

Rahner's theology of death is, then, a consequence of a certain understanding of freedom and time. But does this understanding come from philosophy or Christian revelation? What we have here is not just the more or less successful application of philosophical hypotheses about freedom and the time to revelation. For in discussing these particular understandings of freedom and time, Rahner calls them the *Christian* concepts of freedom and time. In an article on "Christianity and the 'New Man'," for example, he insists that Christianity has "an individual and existential notion of time which is missing in secular utopias."[6] Not that Christian time does not also imply movement toward a societal future, an eschatological city; but at the same time Christianity has an existential concept of time as an *individual* free person's progress toward absolute definitiveness. And this latter conception is the primary one, from which the other is derived.

This existential and individual notion of time Rahner several times characterizes as "Christian." And in his article devoted to the theology of freedom,[7] freedom as the power to realize oneself once and for all is likewise characterized as a Christian idea. Rahner is not merely submitting these ideas as philosophical notions compatible with Christianity, but as ideas already Christian. To establish them he appeals to Scripture, to the complex of statements portraying man as responsible for all of his life before One who looks beneath the surface and reads the heart. Being responsible for the totality of one's life means that this life is the result of one's freedom. In fact, "it is only when this freedom is seen from the vantage point of Christian revelation as deciding absolute salvation or damnation once and for all before God that its real essence finally comes to light."[8] Ordinary everyday

---

6. Karl Rahner, **Theological Investigations,** Vol. V, p. 143.
7. Karl Rahner, **Schriften zur Theologie,** Einsiedeln: Benziger Verlag, 1965, pp. 221-222. This and the following citations through note 9 are all taken from Section Two of the article, "Theologie der Freiheit."
8. **Ibid.,** p. 222.

experience tends to atomize freedom into a series of acts, held together by a neutral substantial self which performs them from time to time. But man's freedom means more than a mere capacity to perform moral acts which then recede into the past but which still can be reckoned to man morally or juridically. From the Christian point of view man disposes over himself in a definitive way, so that as a result of his freedom he *is* good or bad, so much so that his salvation or damnation is already decided. This Christian perspective transforms and deepens the idea of free responsibility. Freedom becomes freedom *to become* oneself and not just *to do* some thing. Choices of individual objects become the concrete material for a more formal, abiding, self-realization before God. This basic self-realization is spread out through time, of course. The total interpretation of oneself, one's fundamental option, which is aimed at in all free acts, remains usually unfilled. In the concrete, then, human freedom is always a unity in difference of this formal and material element, of fundamental option and free individual choice.

A significant thing about this sketch of human freedom is, as we have seen, that Rahner several times labels it Christian. He does not present it merely as a philosophical consideration which can be applied fruitfully to revelation. Actually, philosophy and revelation are here so intertwined that it would be impossible to sort them out and bad theology to try. But, significantly, the one relation of revelation to philosophy that Rahner does mention here is revelation's ability to bring the real essence of freedom to light for the first time. Through revelation the notion of freedom is "transformed and deepened in a remarkable way."[9]

Rahner is much more explicit about the interrelation between philosophy and revelation in the theology of death in his article on "The Life of the Dead," an article that treats death as a person's coming into final maturity.[10] In this article we see him going into as much phenomenological detail as we are ever likely

---

9. **Ibid.**
10. Karl Rahner, **Theological Investigations,** Vol. IV, p. 348.

to get from him, to uncover the exigency for eternity in all radically free acts.

He then stresses once again that since eternity is not just extended time after death, but a kind of freedom, freedom which has been brought to completion in time, eternity can only be understood by a correct grasp of what freedom is. Whereupon he poses the simple question: How do we know all this? How do we know that this fleeting time of ours is really productive of definitive freedom? This question is where the special combination of revelation and man's own knowledge comes in. Revelation calls the human self-understanding (i.e., in this case, the almost universal belief in some sort of life after death) to a more explicit and decided realization of what it already feels in a vague and hesitant way. Rahner proposes to explore the modern version of these ancient beliefs in immortality, the implicit core conviction which still survives the disappearance of the ancient myths. He proposes to retrieve in a modern way this general conviction.

Rahner proceeds by an investigation of acts of love and of moral decision. In such acts, when man is completely authentic, all radical moral cynicism is impossible. At such a moment, one cannot think of the authentic as perishing with time, because it is not temporal. To say to someone, "I love you," is to say, "you shall not die." In moral decision the subject posits itself as definitively valid. It is present to itself as incommensurable with a flow of time that simply drains away. He means, of course, that in the experience of such personal decision one grasps what cannot be drained away by time: the valid. It is not enough to say merely that the idea of moral decision implies eternal validity. One must actually decide. As in all questions of this sort, personal decision and metaphysical insight practically cohabitate. What counts now and forever is spiritual reality. To be a person means to count forever.

This idea is the key to articulating the relation of time and eternity, the key to avoiding the almost inevitable awkward picture of eternity as the linear continuation of time, and death as changing horses for the ride beyond.

To overcome this difficulty we must do what is done in modern physics and learn to think unimaginatively and to this extent perform a process of "de-mythizing." We must say: through death—not after it—*there is* (not: begins to take place) the achieved definitiveness of the freely matured existence of man. What has come to be is there as the hard-won and untrammelled validity of what was once temporal; it progressed as spirit and freedom, in order to be.[11]

Second Approach

If Rahner's first approach to death as act was formal, the second can properly be called existential. It is the approach adopted in his little essay "On Martyrdom," appended to the longer article "On the Theology of Death." One considerable advantage of this shorter exposé is that it leads him to take an existential approach to the voluntary character of death. In the martyrdom article Rahner must show that death is an act, in order to find the intrinsic link between the ideas of "witness" and "death."

Death is an act, something we do. It is certainly also the extreme case of something we merely undergo, something that just happens to us. Rahner makes concessions to the passive nature of death right at the outset, anxious to show that what he means by death as act does not cancel out death as passive. Death as act has more to do with the presence of death throughout life than with the final moment, which is "really the end of death, the death of death," either as "the second death or the killing of death and the victory of life."[12] Because death is continuously present through the whole of human life, biologically and in the concrete experience of each individual person, death is also an act of human freedom.

But the mere presence of death through life does not make death a free act. What must be seen is that man *has* to die his death in freedom. He cannot avoid this death imposed on him as

---

11. **Ibid.**
12. Karl Rahner, **On the Theology of Death,** p. 86.

the task of his freedom. How he dies it, however, how he understands this death, depends on his free decision. His freedom lies
not in the *whether* but in the *how*. One is reminded of James's
arbitration of the Carlyle-Margaret Fuller dispute. One "had
better" accept the universe one finds. But the matter does not
end there. In fact, that is where the matter first begins, the matter
of freedom. "Do we accept it only in part and grudgingly, or
heartily and altogether?"[13] Resignedly or wholeheartedly?

There is a real dialectic of freedom and necessity here, of the
chosen and the imposed. And what is imposed is not just death,
nor the necessity of accepting it just anyhow, but the necessity
of accepting it freely. Man is a tension of person and nature and
by this tension he is obliged, i.e., forced, to come to terms with
death freely, to face it freely. There is no side-stepping the question. This business of being put, unasked, in a situation one must
then accept freely sounds odd, and quite unfair. It should. It makes
no sense at all unless one can get to the very end of it. Being
forced to relate freely to a fact makes no sense unless interpreted
as being asked a question. One can be asked a question unasked.
One cannot be asked a question otherwise; to ask someone's permission to ask him a question is to ask his permission unasked.
Real violence is involved in asking a question. One is forced
to listen. After one has heard it, it is too late not to listen. One
need not answer, however. But if the question is a personal one,
involving one's relationship to the questioner, a response is un-
avoidable. One cannot get off by replying "no comment," because
in such a context any refusal to answer is itself a kind of answer.
By a question of this sort one is quite definitely put in a bind;
one's freedom is being forced. But this is the characteristic of
personal encounters as such. Man is mortal and man is free,
and he is both of these unasked. But in being obliged to die freely,
he is asked how he wills to do this.

This "how" is a question of interpretation, of how man understands the death he must die. "But the question is, how does man

---

13. William James, **The Varieties of Religious Experience,** Westminster, Md.: Modern Library, Inc., 1961, p. 49.

understand this end towards which he freely moves, since he cannot do anything else than run the course of his life in freedom? Does he run protestingly, or lovingly and trustingly? Does he view his end as extinction, or as fulfillment? . . . We must therefore ask what, from the Christian point of view, is this right interpretation of the act of life which is death."[14] "Men do not usually express their answer in abstract statements about death, but they live and tacitly carry out their free conviction through the actions of their life and the deeds of their daily existence, even when they do not know explicitly that by their life they are interpreting their death."[15] Here again we have a reference to the basic option which underlies one's explicit statements, but which is "tacitly" carried out in daily actions, even when one does not explicitly know this. This basic conviction which thus gradually comes to expression in the surface acts and convictions of one's life involves, among other elements, an interpretation of one's own death.

This basic underlying choice is an act of understanding, of interpretation which involves two things. First, it is understanding, existential self-understanding. And secondly, it is a reading of something susceptible to two different but plausible interpretations, something essentially ambiguous. It is an act of understanding, and at the same time an eminently free act. As in our discussion of Rahner's first approach to death as act, we are once again on the deep, unreflexive personal level where freedom and understanding dwell side by side. Such a conception is a key element in existential philosophy, which sees the fundamental human questions as unapproachable by an uncommitted, presuppositionless spectator.

Death is interpretation in the sense of reading a sort of symbol or expression whose meaning is not immediately and unambiguously clear. Does one view his end as extinction or as fulfillment? Death can be viewed in both ways. Does man move "towards a death which is the consummation of vacuity, a final emptying

---

14. Karl Rahner, **On the Theology of Death,** p. 86.
15. **Ibid.**

of life into meaninglessness [or] towards a death which is the valid fulfillment of his existence"?[16] Death itself does not clearly say toward which end we are moving. That death is a fulfillment is not obvious; in fact, death seems to suggest that it is rather the contrary. According to what is most obvious in death, it does not fulfill existence but seems to annihilate it.

Thus Rahner's second approach to death as act comes from a conviction that everything in a person's existence should ultimately be act, should be freely affirmed. Man is basically defined by freedom. Birth, like death, is a free act, in the sense that one must freely assimilate one's de facto origin, that one came into life unasked, that one has a certain factual situation, certain parents, a certain character, a certain prehistory. Even man's freedom, which he discovers as a fact, must be freely assumed. It has to be taken up as a task. The imposed freedom must become a free freedom.

This free acceptance of what is imposed as a fact does not mean accepting it as brute fact. In fact, it means the exact opposite of this. Bowing to brute fact is the precise opposite of freedom; it is freedom surrendering to what is beneath itself. This is what makes Carlyle's retort: "Gad! She'd better," unacceptable.[16a] Free acceptance of what is de facto imposed means making sense of the fact, giving it a meaningful interpretation. Freedom can accept what it can somehow understand. Our earlier statement that dying freely is a question of *how* we die the death we must die in any case, has to be understood with this in mind. The *how*

---

16. Ibid., p. 87.
16a. In a previous chapter of Och's book **The Death in Every Now** he comments: "The willy and the nilly of accepting reality are presented in a classic text from William James's **The Varieties of Religious Experience,** with Margaret Fuller and Thomas Carlyle arguing the points of view of person and nature respectively:

'I accept the universe' is reported to have been a favorite utterance of our New England Transcendentalist, Margaret Fuller; and when someone repeated this phrase to Thomas Carlyle, his sardonic comment is said to have been: 'Gad! She'd better!' "

is not just a question of an accompanying enthusiasm or reluctance, as James almost seems to imply. Acceptance of a brute fact is not more free just because it is enthusiastic, if the enthusiasm is not founded on understanding. Once again we see the convergence of freedom and understanding where radical involvement of the person is concerned. The *how* of our acceptance is then a question of how we interpret what we have to accept. Man's free dying must be "a liberty which says 'yes' not only to death itself, but also to its meaning, to the meaning of human existence."[17]

What death as act, in the meaning accorded it in this second approach, means, can better be seen through consideration of an objection which inevitably comes to mind. The objection is: Must one accept or reject death at all? Must one adopt this existential attitude toward it? Isn't this straining life too much? More precisely, isn't the attitude of "wait and see" more modest, and hence more in tune with life as it is? Or, to put it another way, is there a possible agnostic attitude toward death, an attitude in between interpreting it as the end of it all or the fulfillment of it all? Is there an attitude prior to hope or despair, both of which seem to be quite exalted attitudes, both too ambitious, given the quite banal confusion of human life? How can ordinary people be expected to settle questions about the meaningfulness or meaninglessness of life? Shouldn't we be more *modest* and postpone such interpretations until all the evidence is in? And isn't this the way most people actually live, drifting along, neither accepting the universe nor revolting against it? Can we really believe that people anticipate death to such an extent that their basic choice during life is structured by coming to grips with this awesome reality?

This objection, that there is a kind of limbo between the heaven of hope and the hell of despair, calls for a series of comments, all of which serve to highlight what actually is meant by death as act. First, let us observe that it gives a good illustration of what is meant by regarding death as passive, i.e., it is quite definitely

---

17. Karl Rahner, **On the Theology of Death,** p. 87.

an objection against death as act, for it denies that we need adopt a personal attitude of acceptance or rejection vis-à-vis death. It is saying that death is passive, i.e., something that will happen to us sooner or later but need not concern us now.

The objection makes sense insofar as it succeeds in regarding death as the outcome or issue of life. It misunderstands death as the validation or invalidation of life, death as that which life runs into, the sea into which the river of life flows. Only when this more or less teleological view of death is grasped, does death cast the two contrasting lights on life, that of life running toward fulfillment, toward harvesting all that is in it, toward saving life, toward putting the seal of irrevocable validity on it, or life as ever more manifest futility, ever enclosing captivity, an ever more belied promise. Death is the goal of time, of time as continually gathering or continually draining. But death in either case is the final evaluation of life. "Tell me what you think of death and I will tell you what you think of life." The trouble with the sheer "wait and see" attitude, as when one waits to see whether some future event comes to pass, is that it pretends to a certain indifference about the outcome. It makes the person a spectator at his own destiny, instead of someone committed to a certain issue. Is such indifference really possible? Surely the "wait and see" attitude is not completely indifferent. Complete indifference is really a form of despair, or at least an attitude that has ceased to hope. The degree of indifference or non-commitment here is difficult to characterize, and perhaps we should not call it indifference, because one's own destiny is clearly at stake. What is the difference between the following two attitudes: "I desire fulfillment and fear ultimate frustration"; and "I hope for fulfillment; I do not despair of it." In neither case is there indifference. In the first case, there is a modest wait and see attitude accompanying mere desire and fear. But hope and despair, though they both still have to wait, both do not yet see, yet decide the outcome already. They have pronounced on the issue ahead of time. Need they? Must they? And, if so, what is the type of commitment that means this is so?

So much for one kind of "wait and see" attitude, one that regards death merely as a future moment. But what about the attitude that regards it genuinely as the upshot of life? Can *this* attitude be agnostic? Can an attitude that has already raised itself to the level of hope or despair postpone pronouncement about the outcome? Can it wait until the evidence is in before it commits itself? Or are we on a level where such noncommittal waiting makes no sense?

All the evidence will never be in. Which is to say that the evidence for and against the meaningfulness of life will always remain inconclusive, ambiguous. Life as it appears will never clearly warrant either hope or despair on the basis of evidence. Besides, this kind of evidence is of the sort that depends on an interpretation, evidence that is anything but objective, so that it will be judged positive or negative depending on the judge's prior disposition. Objectively the same picture of life will induce one person to hope, tempt another to despair. So it seems that the prior disposition is all important.

All the evidence will never be in. Then must one withhold judgment? But in the meantime life must be lived. If such questions as the meaningfulness of life cannot receive some answer in this meantime, i.e., while life is actually being lived, then they must be postponed till after life, when the answers are of no more use. But in dealing with questions of hope and despair, of acceptance or flight from life, we are precisely in the realm of basic underlying commitments which govern our interpretation of the evidence. The question comes down to this: does living life in the meantime involve any commitment to life, so that if one refuses such commitment one really belongs to the living dead?

Rahner refers to the realm of such commitments as the realm of the "heart." In using this biblical rubric, Rahner has a definite technical theological notion in mind. It is for him a basic notion fundamental to the study of man. It refers to the center of personal and spiritual disposition over oneself, a center of ourselves that is never completely accessible to us, which can only be approached more and more without ever being really grasped. Yet it is from this dynamic ground that man must look for his basic authentic self-understanding, a self-understanding that he, again, will never completely possess. In this center of the person, understanding and will are still one; neither has precedence over the other. Rahner spells out this primeval unity of understanding and will by listing corresponding pairs of acts in which this mutual priority can better be seen: thought and devotion, understanding and emotion, objectivity and reverence, judgment and persuasion.[18]

It is from this realm, from the center or heart, that man's basic act springs. Whether considered as basically religious, or in its other characteristics as an act of love, or as an act of dying (faith and hope and love as triumphing over the concomitant temptation which death affords), this basic act will have all the peculiarities proper to this deeper realm of the heart.

So much for each of Rahner's two approaches to his statement that death is act. One is formal, the other is existential; one descending, the other ascending. Do they fit perfectly when they meet, one could ask. Since I have already made perhaps too much of the distinction between the approaches, my reply to this question will be a rough list of a few reminders.

One could combine the results of the two approaches roughly as follows: 1. The line between time and eternity is the difference between the effort toward self-appropriation and definitively a- chieved self-appropriation. 2. Though this appropriation of one- self roughly coincides with one's lifetime, because it is the deed of one's lifetime, the line of demarcation does not necessarily coincide with the biological moment of death. 3. In fact, we do not know at what moment our underlying option becomes final. We know only that we are never to consider ourselves confirmed in grace or lost in despair. Concern about the moment is idle (legitimate speculation, perhaps, for a very ontically oriented curiosity); only concern about hope or despair is existential. 4. For all this lack of concern about moments, the connection

---

18. Karl Rahner and Herbert Vorgrimler, **Op. Cit.,** p. 13, Entry: "Act."

between our basic decision and death is by no means arbitrary. One's life is toward death, and the personal appropriation of this life involves coming to terms with death.

Far from attenuating the old Latin phrase *mors certa, hora incerta,* Rahner's theology reaffirms it. It even sharpens it. Death comes like a thief in the night. This biblical image refers primarily to the definitive coming of the Lord. Its application to death is a transferred one which would be illegitimate if death had nothing to do with the Lord's coming. The hour of his coming is uncertain. But when he finally comes, it will be the hour of our "death."

Chapter Eleven

DEATH: A THEOLOGICAL REFLECTION

LADISLAUS BOROS, S.J.

Here we venture on a decisive step towards understanding the mystery of human suffering. At the very heart of the Christian message lies the shattering statement: the real origin of life is death. What happens to man in death is more wonderful than his creation. It is a new birth. But why is this so? Why does life rise out of death? This is the question to which we want to find an answer. The answer runs: Because death offers us the first possibility of making a final decision, face to face with Christ, in complete freedom and with the utmost clarity of mind. Man in death becomes perfectly "person" and therefore only in death can he make a perfect decision. In order to be able to grasp the full import of this assertion, we must first range a little more widely. We must first list the reasons which lead us to say that the real decision of man's life occurs at death.

DEATH AS FINAL DECISION

On the question of the "Last Things" there has been a revolutionary transformation of perspectives in the most recent Catholic theology. Hans Urs von Balthasar rightly described eschatology as the "storm-center of theology." The great change was brought about by raising the quite simple and at first sight insignificant and harmless question: what happens to the whole man at the moment of death? In trying to answer this question, theologians observed that they would have to think out afresh their whole doctrine of the "Last Things" in the light of the answer they gave. The new answer, proposed almost simultaneously by different theologians, might be formulated in this way: in death there emerges the possibility of the first completely personal act of man; hence death is ontologically the favorable point for awareness, for freedom, encounter with God and decision for our eternal destiny.

This statement sounds perhaps a little too academic. What we want to suggest is this: only at the moment of death can man discard the strangeness of his existence; only in death does he become sufficiently master of his being to encounter Christ completely, with every fiber of his nature, and—in that confrontation—to be able finally to make his decision. According to this hypothesis, we would again have a possibility of decision: to be more precise, only in death would we have the first possibility of a complete, fully personal commitment. In this hypothesis, salvation is conceived as radically "Christological" and "personal." And nevertheless it renders intelligible the fact that salvation—brought by Christ and to be won through personal effort by each individual human being—is "universal." In death, confronted by Christ, every man has the opportunity of making his decision in full possession of his powers, in absolute clarity and in complete freedom.

Very much depends on a correct understanding of the expression, "in death," so strongly emphasized in this hypothesis. It is not a question (firstly) of the state "before death." We cannot really assume that someone posits his first completely personal act in a state of agony of body and soul, in the stupor of dying. But neither is it a question (secondly) of the state "after death." Our eternal destiny is forever fixed after death. In death we have become "final" to such an extent that afterwards nothing can be altered in this finality. It is in fact a question here of the "moment of death itself."

Moment of Encounter with Christ

The protagonists of this theory conceive the moment of death in the following way: when the soul leaves the body, it awakens suddenly to its pure spirituality, is wholly filled with light and brightness. It understands instantaneously all that a created spirit can know and understand; it sees its whole life concentrated into a unity; it discovers therein Christ's call and leadership; it stands also before the wholeness of the world and sees how the risen Lord shines out there as the world's ultimate mystery. In death, therefore, man becomes free, aware and capable of making a final decision; in this decision he accomplishes the clearest encounter of his life with Christ; it is now impossible for him to pass Christ by. He must decide, this way or that. What is decided there—in death—remains for eternity, since man throws his whole nature into this decision, becomes wholly decision. As so decided, he lives for ever. The whole of man's eternity will be nothing but the ontological unfolding of what took place in that moment.

The arguments brought forward in support of this doctrine cannot be analyzed individually here. But to indicate the general line of thought, we may point to one consideration. These theologians appeal to a profoundly human experience: man does not yet "possess" himself. In his longing, he never ceases to live ahead of himself and is therefore nowhere able to pin himself down, to give himself a final shape; in order to be, he stumbles ahead into time; thereby he merely skirts—so to speak—his present moment, the "point" at which he is really "there"; he merely skirts his own life and does not really live it. He cannot unfold his nature, cannot live his life in all its richness wholly and undividedly.

Only in the moment when it is impossible to go further into the same, fragmented future, can he fully realize his nature. Here

the streams of his life meet together. He "is" finally; he no longer
lives like a rushing mountain brook, but like a calm mountain
lake, clear and deep, reflecting the whole world in its profusion.
But this moment can occur only in the moment of death. For only
in death can there simply be no more "further" in the same direction, into the empty openness of time: in death a new life dawns
for us, which is the unceasing, intensively lived present. Only
in death, therefore, does man reach the total unity of his being;
he gets away from the universal constriction and unease and
enters into the depths of the world, into the "heart of the universe."

"New Birth"

If we want to describe the event of death pictorially in the
light of this hypothesis, then the ancient Christian symbol for
death—the analogy of birth—suggests itself. At birth, the child
is thrust violently—so to speak—out of the narrow space of the
mother's womb; it must leave the protecting, familiar, secure
shelter. It is abandoned to a complete "breakdown." Simultaneously there lies open a vast, new world, a new relation to the
world, the world of light, colors, meanings, the world of being
with others and of love. In death something similar happens to
man: he is taken out violently from the narrow space of his
previous worldliness; at the same time he enters into a new, essential relation to the world, extending into the vastness of the universe. In death therefore, on the one hand, man really "goes
under," in the sense that there is a "nullifying," a violent with-
drawal of his bodily worldliness; at the same time, he plunges
down to the roots of the world and acquires a total presence to
the world.

This ground of the world, to which man descends as he dies,
is of its nature "open to Christ," transparent therefore to the
ground of all that is. Man in death is also confronted with what
he always surmises in all his knowing, that towards which he unconsciously strives in all his willing, what he embraces in reality
in all his loving. At this metaphysical center he will make his

final decision. Death, therefore, is birth. Man in his death enters a world wholly radiant with Christ. The cosmic Christ completely envelops it. In his whole being man stands before his Lord. He can no longer pass him by.

"Liberation to Freedom"

Man must go through death in order to come in his wholeness close to God. During our earthly life we are still wandering at a distance from true reality. We are dominated by people, things and events, by our own longings and dreams. All this fills up space, within and without, draws man into its power. This multiplicity of things scarcely leaves space for God any longer in our thoughts. If he is to enter heaven, the possibility must be open to man—wholly independent and free, with his whole human reality led back as it were to the essentials of his being—of one day standing before God and deciding for him with his whole nature. But for this to take place, everything must be taken away from him to which he clings with every fiber of his reality. His things, his possessions, his power, even his friends, people dear to him, his hopes and dreams, all that he has built up and achieved in his life. One day all masks must fall, all roles too must come to an end: all the parts that man plays before the world and before himself.

By experiencing death, therefore, man is liberated from everything that prevented him hitherto from seeing God face to face. Death therefore is liberation to true freedom. Through death man is delivered up completely to his God. He cannot any longer hide himself from God. His soul is—so to speak—transplanted into that infinite field where there is nothing but himself and his God. He stands now face to face with the risen Lord. Christ himself had to make his own the death-struggle, dying and death, so that every man who goes on the way of death might meet him suddenly in blinding clarity, so that every man—at least in death—would make a final decision, face to face with him.

Irrevocable Decision

Here—in death—God has completely overtaken man. By taking death on himself, he has closed up all ways of escape. Man has to go through death. And in death he will meet Christ irrecusably. Here the terrible adventure of keeping at a distance from God—comes to its end. Christ is now standing there, before man in death: clearly seen, luminously perceived, he calls man to himself with the gesture of redeeming love.

Christ will for ever stand there, his love calling and seeking to give itself. If man in death decides against Christ, it makes no difference to Christ's love. But this love will burn him eternally, because he eternally experiences it as utterly close and nevertheless rejects it (and this is hell). But if he decides for Christ, then the same love of Christ becomes for him eternal light and final perfection in infinite happiness, the eternal acceptance of the closeness of our Lord (heaven). Thus the decision in the moment of death is the judgment itself.

Death as the "Particular Judgment"

By his Yes or No man finally passes judgment on himself. It follows from this: No one is damned merely because chance so brought it about, merely because—perhaps as a result of an accident—he was suddenly called away into eternity; because he had never properly known God during his earthly life, because he was born into a family where he never had any experience of love and therefore also could not understand what is God's nature; because he perhaps turned against a God in whom he saw merely a legalistic God, a ferocious tyrant; because he was abandoned by men, misunderstood and inwardly wounded, and thus turned in rebellion against everything, even against God. Anyone who thinks otherwise does not know what eternal self-damnation is.

It follows from this: No one attains eternal salvation merely because he had pious parents; because his middle-class prejudices prevented him from doing the evil he would so much have liked to do; because he had the chance, which billions of men—perhaps better men than he—do not have, of growing up in a part of the world where, at least occasionally, something may still be heard about Christ; because he happened to have a pleasant manner and thus also knew what it means to be loved and did not find it difficult to believe that God also loved him. Anyone who thinks otherwise does not know what eternal "deifying" means.

It follows from this: God is not small-minded; he is a truly great Lord. We are not damned unless we have decided against Christ, with our whole nature, in complete clarity and with full reflection; but neither are we deified unless we have embraced Christ in an intimate encounter, with all the fibers of our soul. Where we were born, where we died, what kind of character we inherited, all this is completely irrelevant; every man has the possibility of deciding in blinding clarity, for or against Christ. Man is not the toy of a "small and mean" God. Such a "God" does not exist.

It follows from this: Every man has the possibility, at least once, of meeting Christ, the Risen One, of knowing him personally; even the heathen, those billions who have not yet heard of Christ; even Christians who have become heathens, to whom perhaps we have preached a God who is boring and remote from reality, a God whom they could never learn properly to love; even those human beings who have simply remained small children in matters of religion and morality, although the rest of their capacities developed in a thoroughly normal way and they were able to make their way successfully in the complex structure of modern life; even those human beings who hate God, because they see in him —for example—an instrument of "capitalist exploitation" and have never known him in his true nature; even the mentally defective and emotionally immature, who were never able to understand anything properly; even the unborn and children who died without baptism; finally, we ourselves who are too weak to do what is good and whose hearts remain so cold and empty. In the light of our proposed hypothesis, all have the possibility of gaining their salvation in a completely personal encounter with Christ.

It follows from this: We must all remain alert. What and who gives us the assurance that we shall make the right decision in death? The outcome of this decision will depend on ourselves. There is no other standard by which to judge the sincerity of our conversion except conversion itself at this moment. What we want to be in the future, we must begin in the present. We must prepare ourselves by the many small, individual decisions of our life for the great, final decision in death. Life is "practice for the judgment." We must convert ourselves—and, indeed, at once—if we sincerely want conversion in death. Any postponement of this pre-decision is an existential lie. We simply cannot go on living thoughtlessly and leave everything over to the final decision. Who can guarantee that we shall again at the end overturn the whole orientation of our lives? Only we ourselves. The idea of a possible final decision in death is like all great Christian ideas: it liberates and at the same time imposes demands. The proposed hypothesis offers us the possibility of understanding the "particular judgment," not as an item added to the long list of so-called "Last Things," but as a dimension of the decision in death, as the final determination of our nature. It remains to be seen whether the same argument will be successful also in the question of purgatory.

DEATH AS PURGATORY

The hypothesis of the ultimate decision in death permits us to get rid of some incredible, unworthy and grotesque ideas of purgatory. The place of purification is certainly not a gigantic city of torment, a 'cosmic concentration camp,' in which wailing, groaning and moaning creatures are punished by God. God's thoughts have a very different greatness. Purgatory could certainly be conceived as an instantaneous event, as the quality and intensity of the decision formed in death. In this case the encounter with Christ, the entry before his loving gaze, would be our final purgation.

Purgatory as Encounter with Christ

With love and grace Christ looks on the person who is approaching him. But his gaze simultaneously penetrates to the innermost recesses, the most hidden places, and to what is most essential in human existence. To encounter God in the fiery gaze of Christ is indeed, on the one hand, the supreme fulfillment of our capacity to live; but, on the other hand, it is also the most terrible suffering of our nature. In this perspective, purgatory would be nothing but the passage through the fire of Christ's love, the event of the encounter with Christ in death. In this encounter, love for God breaks out of the depths of human existence and penetrates our whole nature. To do this, it must break down the layers and "deposits" of selfishness—what scholastic theology calls *reliquiae peccati,* "the remains of sin." Love for God does indeed still glow in the depth of that human soul which is in need of purification; but it is buried under the dust and ashes of man's egoism. The harder and more solid these deposits are, the more painful also will be the breakthrough to Christ. Man's whole existence must "break out" with its last resources, open itself to the loving approach of Christ. According to this theory, then, individual human beings in the moment of death would go through a process of purgation, varying in intensity with each person. Thus, instead of a difference in the time spent in purgatory, there would be a difference in the intensity of purgation.

Our Sustaining Intercession

At this point the objection may be raised: "If purification in purgatory is an instantaneous event, why then should we pray for our dead? In any case, our prayer arrives too late." Two different answers can be given to this objection. The one is philosophical, drawn from the concept of temporality. We shall leave this on one side. The other answer, the more important and decisive, is theological.

For God all is present: for him our prayer and the death of the person for whom we are praying coincide; for him, the human being whom we love and whose decision we want to make easier by the support of our prayer is dying at the moment when we are praying for him. The situation is of course similar to that which holds in the widespread devotional exercise in honor of the Sacred Heart, the "Holy Hour." By their prayer and compassion, the faithful comfort their Savior in the Garden of Gethsemane, in his human sorrow and dread. And this consolation really "consoles," since for God the two points of time exist simultaneously. Our intercession therefore can never arrive "too late," since God by his very nature knows no before and after. Our aid to the deceased person always arrives at the right moment, even if we are praying for him decades after his death. His moment is always simultaneously our moment. His decision always occurs now, even if he long ago attained eternal bliss. At every moment of our time we can sustain him in the greatest decision of his life. Our theory of purgatory therefore in no way depreciates the devout intercession of the faithful, but gives a more profound, more human dimension.

DEATH AS A POSSIBILITY OF SELF-DAMNATION

Here we must reflect prayerfully—albeit very briefly—on one of the darkest mysteries of our existence, on the possibility of hell. We know from revelation that this possibility lies open to all of us. But the same revelation forbids us to assume of any concrete individual that he has in fact been abandoned to hell.

Inviolability of Freedom

Christ repeatedly and emphatically forbade us to condemn any human being. To the sinful woman he said: "Neither do I condemn you" (Jn 8:11). Man therefore is not an "object of judgment," not even of the judgment of Christ. Only man can condemn himself. Damnation is never anything other than self-damnation. Christ is content simply to reveal his love. In face of this love, man must pass judgment on himself. Whoever utters in death the Yes of his life is not condemned. But whoever says 'No' to Christ's love has already condemned himself. Any kind of judgment on Christ's side, therefore, becomes superfluous. Judgment is nothing but the revelation of love and man's decision in face of this love.

If we try to penetrate further into this complex, we notice that something final and definitive is stated here about man. There is in man a sacred "reserve," which even Christ will not infringe. In this reserve—which is nothing other than the radical freedom of the creature—a creature of God, even when it has fallen away from God, may not be disturbed. Any kind of dishonoring of freedom would be an insult to God, the Creator of this freedom. Is this not the meaning of the mysterious statement in the Epistle of Jude, "when the archangel Michael, contending with the devil, ... did not presume to pronounce a reviling judgment upon him" (verse 9)? Peter's Second Epistle even calls the fallen angels "the glorious ones," against whom "angels before the Lord do not pronounce a reviling judgment" (2:10-11). Freedom, any kind of freedom, represents an absolute in the world. But the absolute is simply untouchable, not to be manipulated. Not even God can do anything if a creature—for instance, man in death—tells him to his face: "No." In this consists the glory, but also the awful menace of our freedom.

Damnation, Self-chosen Separation from God

With his "No" uttered in the presence of Christ, clearly known and revealed in love, man hurls himself into eternal abandonment. In death man becomes wholly "himself," completely overtakes himself and is thus able—as he was not able during his earthly life—to express his nature perfectly in an act of his whole being. If at this moment of the clearest freedom he says his "No," then he says it with his whole nature, hardens himself completely in his denial; indeed, he himself becomes wholly and absolutely denial. He chooses himself for ever: he must therefore endure himself eternally, must grope around for all eternity, lost in the dark void of his own existence.

It is not as if Christ would close up against him the "way out." Christ receives his creature with love whenever and wherever the latter comes to him. Our Lord rejects no one. Hell is not simply a punishment for a past sin (now perhaps bitterly repented). It is sin absolutely speaking, an always present sin, accepted with the whole of a man's nature. It is the rejection of Christ's love, unceasing flight from God. If God were to cease to love the person who thus damns himself, hell too would instantly cease to be hell. But God cannot do otherwise than love. His nature consists in love. His love is perfectly independent of the way in which the creature responds to it. We cannot force God not to love. If at any moment, therefore, the damned person were to repent of his deed of self-damnation he would there and then be in heaven. But that is just what he will not do. And in that refusal his hell consists.

This self-chosen separation from God causes in the person who freely damns himself a profound conflict: an inward cleavage and a state of hostility to the world as a whole. These divisions serve to explain all the pains of hell, which are summed up by theologians under the concepts of *poena damni* (pain of loss) and *poena sensus* (pain of sense).

Separation from God: when we lose God, the eyes become blind to beauty, to life, to richness, to true reality.

Separation from oneself: the nature of the created spirit consists in the fact that it longs for God with its whole reality; separation from God therefore occasions in it a cleavage reaching down to its innermost being; the damned person hates what is most real in his own nature, that which makes him long for God.

Separation from the world as a whole: the world consists in God's love given bodily shape in the creature; creation everywhere bears the image of that which the damned person radically denies; man also is substantially planted into the world; he embodies the universe in himself. The damned person then lives in a world which he feels to be his enemy, which everywhere burns him, resists him; and this burning—since man bears the world within himself—penetrates to the most hidden fibers of human reality.

Imprisoned in the Self in the midst of a World radiant with God

From all this it follows that hell is not a "special place," but the same world in which the blessed also live in eternal happiness.

God cannot in fact deliberately create an "evil place." By his very nature, he is incapable of doing that. If God creates anything, it is bound to be good, since God can allow something to come to be only by fashioning it according to his nature; if it were not made in his image, it would simply be a non-entity. But the damned are simply out of place in this world.

Imagine a day when the sky is blue, the sun embraces the world in its rising morning glow, the birds sing, man is utterly happy. What harmony, what joy! But take a fish out of the water to enjoy this wondrous beauty: for the fish it is hell. And that is how the damned person lives unhappily in a world utterly radiant with God. According to some biblical accounts (particularly in the Book of Job and in the Prophet Zechariah), the blessed and the damned live in the same place, in the same world, associate with one another and have the right to talk with God. In fact, it could not be otherwise. If it were, the damned would not suffer at all in their separation from God, from themselves and from the world; their state would certainly not be that which they established for eternity by their absolutely free "No" in death.

We have thus tried to explain hell as the "No" of the decision in death turned into an eternal state, therefore as a dimension of death itself. The same holds—of course, with the tokens reversed—for heaven. In uttering "Yes" with his whole being in death, man overcomes the terror of encountering God (purgatory), outstrips everything which in God is perilous to our finite nature. Man can now enter into the knowledge and into the love of Christ, which in fact is the very essence of heaven. It follows that heaven is nothing other than the decision for Christ turned into a state of being.

Instead of spending longer on the discussion of this hypothesis about death, we would like now to present an imagined experience of what may happen to us at death. We ought to try for once to imagine our own death. We have therefore composed this last part of our discussion in the first person. The individual pictures which occur in it are of course merely pictures and therefore are not to be understood as literally true.

DEATH AS A SOURCE OF LIFE

I am now lying there, on my death-bed, limp, weary and unable to move my limbs. I listen to the blood rushing in my veins, throbbing in my ears. Marvellous music of life which becomes more and more remote. Dimly I still see the world through purple veils, my eyes red with fever. Weariness vibrates in my whole nature and blots out the familiar faces of the world. Exhaustion becomes more and more dominant. I have no longer sufficient strength to break through the wall of my solitude.

Abandoned in Human Solitude

I have now become finally alone. Alone as never before in my life. The loved ones around me have to look on, inactive and powerless, while I am being driven into an inescapable whirlpool of solitude. Snatched away into unrelieved loneliness, departed to the furthest outposts of the world. That is what my dying means. I can no longer even cry for help. I am powerless, bewildered, helpless as a child confined in a dark place. I have been hurled into the great, gray mist of infinite distance, into unmoving, muted, silent helplessness. The things and people in my life suddenly cease to exist.

I plunge more and more deeply into the misty darkness. Where, in fact, am I being hurled? Out beyond all earthly shores. But the amazing thing is that I do not find it strange to be hurled out in this way. I am plunging into something I have always known. It is as if I already once experienced this—and, indeed, not only once, but often in my life. I am being carried away to where I have always been in my dreams, in my longings, to that region which I have always divined behind things, persons and events.

This perception now strikes me with singular clarity. All around me now is light. The dominion of darkness has now ceased. Everything that I ever wanted in my life is now here. Here there awaits me the first smile that I ever perceived on the face of someone I loved. Here there awaits me that greatness which I sought in love, fatherhood, motherhood and friendship. Here await me the rough affection of my father, the tender look of my mother. All this now becomes one, submerged in a wondrous light, a light that does not dazzle but heals. Everything is here. All that was beautiful and precious on earth I find here again. Everything merges into one, marvelously radiant; everything glows, beats like a single heart; everything surges and blazes up. I am at last at home and hold fast the universe.

I plunge into the sacrament of death, in which all individual sacraments are comprised. Everything here is cleansing water, crystal-clear, life-giving, and I am immersed into this fount of being. Everything here is the rustling wind of the Spirit, telling me of mysteries of which my heart never dreamed. Everything here is marvellous food, bread of life, blood of the Lord, fortifying and nourishing. Everything here is penitence and pardon. Everything here is spiritual power, commanding the world's adoration. Everything here is unction, peace, strengthening, satisfaction and homecoming. Here already, I was always at home. This was the one thing shining in the depths of all my dreams and desires.

Becoming One with the World in Christ

Behind this luminous creatureliness, into which I now plunge as I am dying, God himself now begins to shine out. My heart has now ceased to beat. But in the meantime I gained the heart of the universe. In my heart the whole world is concentrated. I am now standing face to face with the risen Lord, since everything around me and in me has become wholly transparent to him. This is the moment for which I have been secretly waiting during my whole life. I now utter the one word of which my love is still capable and which sums up my whole life, the dreams of mankind and the longing of the universe: "Thou." Out of that word there grows an eternal embrace. Out of the mighty destiny of death I make a personal decision of love. Out of abandonment to Christ I make a devotion which draws me into Christ himself.

This is God's moment. He thought of this moment already, billions of years ago, when he created the world. He thought of it at every stage of the slowly ascending evolution of the world. He thought of it when he prepared his own coming, during the time he spent as a stranger, forsaken and unnoticed in a remote corner of our world. He thought of it during his terrible agony, in his death, when he broke through the wall of worldliness; in his descent, in what we call the descent into hell, when he entered into the heart of the world; in his resurrection and ascension, in which he filled the universe.

He went through all that and took it on himself, so that I might meet him, now in death, in the depths of the universe and of my own being, and utter the word full of love: "Thou." Saying "thou" then snatches me out of my nothingness and creates new being in me. A new corporality arises in me, no longer imprisoned within myself but embracing the universe. Now I see everything again with bodily eyes: I see God and also all that I left behind me. Everything now is infinitely close to me and I embrace mysteriously all those who are around me, mourning; those too who are with God, awaiting me.

A new state of the world, which is called "heaven," is opening out before me. Only now, after boldly and extravagantly making over my nature to Christ and thus gaining eternal happiness, do I realize with a new force how terrible, how annihilating was the other possibility on which I might have decided. If in death I had rebelled against this divine "Thou," as Satan did, at the beginning out of sheer hatred thrusting God away from himself eternally, then I would have plunged into infinite solitude, into the choking gloom of confinement within myself, into self-damnation.

I become utterly calm and silent, losing myself in gratitude for the gift of the triune God: the eternally enduring gift of his love. An eternity which is an ever-new beginning, everlasting transfiguration, lies before me: a state of the world become one in love. Hence death is truly the peak of world-events, the source of eternal life. In it man plunges more steeply than can be conceived into unfathomable depths, but only in order to mount up again and surge over, like a rising breaker, into eternal consummation.

Chapter Twelve

THE MYSTERY OF DEATH

ROGER TROISFONTAINES, S.J.

If we desire to discover the meaning of any given reality, the best way is by "living" it. In the case of death, of course, we are faced with a unique situation. Death is the one experience we are absolutely certain not to escape. Yet when the experience does arrive there will be no time left for any description. We never are in a position to describe from within the phenomenon called "death." Nevertheless, our search for its sense does not necessarily mean groping about in complete darkness. As a matter of fact, the direction of any curve indicates the position of its asymptote. Death is the last act, the terminating act of life. Perhaps we can find its meaning if we can manage to discover the law of what I could call the vital curve.

What is *the meaning of human life?* What is its essential trend, discernible behind the multitude of the capricious intricacies of our destiny? It would seem that we can distinguish *two main curves.*

The first and most evident curve is precisely the one that makes the question inevitable. We witness the irreversible running down, from conception to death, of a certain energy potential. This energy is utilized, first, in the prodigious task of building a body, starting with the fertilized ovum, and ending with a finished framework composed of thousands of millions of diversified cells. The same power also feeds the multiple functions of the organism. But it is being spent faster than it can be replenished; and as the supply dwindles, the body stiffens more and more. There is a marked difference between a young child and an old man, in resilience, capacity of adaptation, and general vitality in every sphere. If there were no other curve besides this first one, human life would be nothing but the history of a progressive sclerosis and degradation.

But the decrease of the bodily power is not an unqualified loss. The same power source, at least up to the threshold of old age, supplies another kind of energy. The curve of the latter, running counter to that of the body, indicates the increasing possibility of a more extensive, but also more intimate participation, and of an ever more conscious and free involvement—or a refusal. Whatever the connection of the first curve with the second, the latter certainly deserves our full attention.

What do we mean by *participation* and *involvement?* The human being is always defined by his relative position in a geographical, temporal, racial, affective, personal, political, ideological, religious environment. He *participates*. This participation, however, takes place on a variety of *successive levels*. At the beginning, the individual finds himself passively involved in his environment. He plays no active part in his own conception; and for years he will live in almost total ignorance and dependence. As he gradually begins to grow up, we notice the following things:

his actions come more and more from within him;
the environment that once held him so tightly now widens;
his self-consciousness is deepening;
he realizes more and more his capacity for personally determining the type of relationship he desires to maintain with his own given situation.

That is what active involvement means. Let us examine briefly each of these aspects.

First Aspect: *Growing Activity*

As the various psychic functions appear and develop one after the other, they normally enable the individual to act in an ever more powerful and co-ordinated manner. Many stages of development separate the first reflex action and elementary emotional reaction from the perfect bodily mastery displayed by an athlete, a dancer, a yogi; from the artisan's skill, the initiative of the business executive or that of a head of a state; from artistic creation, motherly or married love, and mystical prayer. The individual continues to grow through countless vicissitudes, and that in spite of apparent recessions. But we cannot help being struck that *this growth is especially stimulated by trial*.

As the circumstances keep changing, the individual is forced to modify the attitude he maintained towards previous situations: he must react, adapt himself, improvise, and create. When a baby is born, after nine months in his mother's womb, he must, under pain of death, open his lungs to the free inrush of oxygen; his first cry is the prelude to autonomous respiration. From now on, he must regulate his bodily temperature, and he must suck to feed himself. In return he will soon discover the sweetness of motherly care, the cosy warmth of clothing and equally that of a bath, the taste of milk as it fills his little mouth, the bliss of having a full stomach, the music of voices, then the glory of lights and colors . . . all the marvels of human experience.

No one asked him if he wanted to be expelled from the comfortable situation in which he had first grown. Luckily so. For supposing it were possible to consult him, would he not, perhaps, have clung with all the stubborn determination of his ignorant passivity to the silent darkness of his prison, to the umbilical cord through which he was being fed? Psychoanalysts tell us that some people—those who did not pass the trial of birth with complete success—unconsciously yearn for the golden age, the blissful inactivity of prenatal life.

Trial is a blessing; and the constant change of circumstances is an absolute condition of growth. But it is the individual's responsibility to react to the various elements he is faced with, and to find, in an increasingly active manner, his own equilibrium in the new surroundings. A thousand and one times, throughout his life, he will have to make similar efforts to set up new methods of approach, adapt himself to the circumstances and use them as occasions for his relentless growth.

Second Aspect: Widening of Environment

A closer look will convince us that the phenomenon of "birth" repeats itself over and over again. A human being is constantly faced with the task of leaving a former situation wherein he has grown and enjoyed a certain equilibrium, and entering another wider set of circumstances where he finds less external security.

Upon leaving the womb, a suckling still lives as a parasite. Weaning—or rather a series of weanings—forces him to forgo certain aspects of the bodily presence of his mother, and to get accustomed to a variety of foods. At about the same age, a baby begins to explore his clothes, his body, and everything else within reach and sight. No sooner is he able to crawl than he sets out to conquer space. Soon he will toddle about, and discover house, staircase, garden and street. So far, however, all his experiences occur within the family. His home is like a psychic transposition of the umbilical cord. The first day in school is truly like a new birth. The child steps from one nursery environment into another, wider and more indifferent, but also one wherein his sensibility, imagination and developing mind find a richer sustenance. High school, military service, college, graduate school, professional career, or civic responsibility will also give rise to similar crises.

The horizon itself, first confined to the street or to the neighborhood, will gradually include city, country, the whole world . . . to the moon and the stars.

History, too, which used to mean more to us than the present moment, has gradually become a limitless panorama. Whichever way we turn, the visible world eludes our attention and stretches indefinitely into the invisible.

As the sphere of knowledge expands, so also does that of love, which sheds the indispensable but temporary protective shells one after the other.

Every instance of weaning may still be felt as a painful separation. But were not such pain imposed upon us, or proposed to our free acceptance, what would we know of the happiness contained in love?

Third Aspect: *Deepening of Consciousness*

Consciousness deepens in the exact rhythm in which the environment widens. This interdependence is by no means accidental. Everything we know or love is at first a relationship whose terms will be distinguished and opposed only later. In the primordial nebula where consciousness is born there is yet no subject, neither "I" nor "you." Only when a baby is capable of recognizing external objects as independent bodies does he recognize himself as a limited body. The self begins truly to be distinguished and felt only when "others" become independent entities. The words "myself," or "I," which the child has used before by pure imitation, now acquire an entirely new meaning for him. He feels the value of his "yes," and still more, it seems, of his "no," which is more liable to cause a reaction and stresses his autonomy. The child knows himself mainly from the other's viewpoint; he discovers himself in the eyes and the judgment of those around him, much as he does when he makes faces in front of a mirror. His reaction, however, is still superficial.

The first friendship, the first love when he is adolescent, suddenly reveal to his eyes the inscrutable depths of his own self and that of the other person; he becomes aware of closeness heretofore unsuspected and yet accessible. The "me" becomes a true "I" exactly at the same instant as the other person, the "he" or "she," becomes for me that unique "you" to whom I both open out and give myself.

As we have seen, the consciousness not only discovers and explores the multiple dimensions of the universe and of the mind, but in search of his own self undertakes a pilgrimage along which countless trials lie in wait for him, a pilgrimage whose goal he will never reach.

Fourth Aspect: Progressive Liberation

As knowledge and self-consciousness gradually develop, they reveal to the individual the resilience of the various components of a situation, as well as his own transcendent role in building up those components. Framework and signification come from the subject. As children, each of us used to find a lot of pleasure in looking at the pattern of a pavement, that of a rug or even of a window pane, and, by so doing, "conjuring up" various forms and designs which changed according to our imagination. Technical inventions, practical ideas in business or in the social field, scientific hypotheses, artistic creation, political ideology, choice of a partner in love, philosophical systems—in all these things subjective construction has a tremendous and overgrowing importance. The elements are given, but it is consciousness that marshalls them, synthesizing them in a completely original manner which we are compelled to call *creation* in the human sense of the word.

Man applies this creative power not only to things and ideas, but also and primarily, in building his own self. Psychic security, which at first had to be supported from the outside, becomes more and more an inner issue, just as bodily balance has been. A normal man is a being who progressively shapes his own personality. He is free; more precisely he *becomes* free.

As a matter of fact, human life contains the inner rhythm of constantly renewed possibilities and acts of self-realization. Nobody chose to exist. Thrown into this adventure of life, the human being is carried by the pre-existing currents of heredity, family, society. Soon, however, he emerges high enough above these currents to accept or fight the obscure forces, to weigh them one against the other, divert and modify them, making use of their power to his own personally determined ends.

This transition from the state of "imposition" to that of "freedom" is perceivable especially at the age of puberty. As a rule, a child is well balanced, reasonable. Almost every teenager is a being disproportioned in body, imagination, mind, and emotions. He questions every value known to him. Childish grace has disappeared together with the former equilibrium. But if the crisis ends well, is there a greater beauty than that of youthful manhood or womanhood wherein a healthy body, a well-trained mind, a personal morality and religion are all synthetized in peaceful harmony? The difference—and the progress—stem from this: that the equilibrium of the child is passively accepted, and is characterized by ignorance and immunization, whereas the balance acquired by the adult, if he comes out victoriously from the crisis of puberty, is an *active* one, reconquered by an effort that is, at least in part, personal. When a human being finally reaches maturity, what truly defines him is not his birth and other exterior circumstances, but his own personal value, his active conduct, his own family and professional career.

A man thrown into this world is like a plane catapulted into the air: he is launched by an external force, but then he must fly under his own power. The inner self must take over from the outside forces, and this remodelling, re-creating of one's creative being is a never-ending task. At the final stage I shall *be* only what my response will have made of me. Now, the more I advance, the more clearly I discover myself capable of an ever more intimate and active involvement both with my own self and with an environment whose limits continue to widen. But, to the extent that I become aware of my freedom, I realize that I am also free to reject these relationships, capitulate in face of trials and failure, and lock myself up in sullen or haughty isolation.

Does not the curve below indicate *the direction* each destiny on earth follows or at least enters upon? Does not the law we are seeking, the permanent structure, the meaning of life, consist in man's for ever binding *obligation to tear himself away, willingly or reluctantly, from an environment where his equilibrium was more passive, more external, and to enter into a vaster and more complex new situation, where he is bound to fail unless he penetrates more and more deeply into his own self and is united ever more intimately to the being he discovers step by step?*

None of us would hesitate to answer "yes" to the above question if we were to stop at the threshold of old age.

But the slackening off we observe at that age seems to be attributable to the meeting of two curves. The bodily energy (curve A) decreases to the point where it can no longer supply adequate power to psychic and spiritual life (curve B). The body, which formerly was a necessary condition of personal activity, in the end becomes a hindrance.

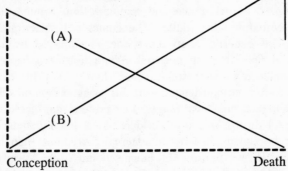

Conception   Death

Similar situations are often found at earlier stages as well. The womb, which was an absolute condition for life during the prenatal period, becomes an obstacle (and is, no doubt, obscurely felt as such) the moment that the human being is about to be born. The same thing happens to the successive, ever-widening substitute for the womb, like the mother's lap, home, family, school, group, or country. We have seen that a human being grows and attains higher stages precisely by the very fact of tearing himself away from previous environments which have become like so many prisons.

If we consider life as a series of births, the analogies of various situations suggest we accept the following hypothesis, which helps to locate the asymptote of the vital curve. *Is it not true that death is another birth?* Is not this present body, whose power is constantly diminishing, an indispensable but only provisional womb? Has it not to be relinquished if the person, developed thanks to its functioning, is to be born?

If we are not sure of immortality, the study of these two curves, which in human life cross each other, could supply a strong indication that personal activity will not perish. If we do believe in immortality, the hypothesis that there remains a certain activity within the very phenomenon called "death" appears almost as an absolute certainty. Is it possible to suppose between two active stages there is an intermediate stage of complete passivity? Could the passivity we observe be anything else but the husk surrounding the ripe fruit? It is only normal that the person, as long as he is tied to the present body, should suffer because of the physiological decay. But if the values the person himself has acquired are indestructible, the person simply waits until this painful process of dying ends, and then he begins to display his own potentialities.

Seen from this angle, old age is not in contradiction with the general movement of life. Being undoubtedly the preface of death, it displays only the reverse of the medal: the abandonment of a formerly sustaining but now strangling environment. The foetus is subjected to the most painful crisis of its prenatal life precisely when it is about to be born: it is squeezed, constricted, almost strangled, and finally expelled, with no knowledge for it of free air, space, light and love awaiting it beyond the passage. Immediately before death, this other great passage, man suffers biological dissolution. As Shakespeare expressed it: "He shuffles off this mortal coil." With no experience of what he is about to become, he fights for air and feels as if he were being expelled from his body. It is clear, therefore, that the positive meaning of this event cannot be revealed by the preparatory phase, the expulsion: the pains of birth are not yet birth itself, and old age and dying are not yet the stage at which the spiritual person is delivered from the material body.

What happens at the moment, not of apparent or "clinical" death, but at the moment of real and absolute death?

This decisive experience cannot be described in earthly language. As long as we are only onlookers, we learn nothing but the negative aspect of departure. The body, left to itself, becomes once again mere matter, passive and reduced to its elements. But could we not suppose that the spiritual self, now freed from this matter, is in a position to carry out without hindrance the activities proper to it? The entire logic of human development strongly suggests that the departing person is at the threshold of an adventure in which his activities, now more conscious and freer than ever, turn toward a limitless horizon. That is the substance of the hypothesis on death which we are about to describe. We follow the same pattern as was adopted for our consideration of the vital curve.

First Aspect: Growing Activity

From the instant of conception, the activity-passivity balance tips more and more heavily in favor of the activity side. We have pointed out that a mature man is defined not so much by what he passively receives as by what he achieves in the world, and most of all in himself. But however deep this action may reach, he has no choice but to work with all his potentialities as well as his inherited weaknesses. To be fully active, to become truly what his own acts make him, he should have the opportunity of choosing freely the kind of body he thinks would fit him, and to determine in full independence the type of relationships he wishes to maintain with other beings. *Departure from the material body* in which passivity prevails *would appear as a necessary condition of full activity*. This departure is precisely the most evident aspect of every death. As a butterfly leaves the cocoon in which it has developed as a chrysalis, as the foetus breaks the amnion at birth, so also, when we step into the final state of our destiny, we leave this present body which has been the primary condition of our personal ripening.

That does not mean that we are about to become disincarnate spirits. The phenomenological view we have thus far adopted clearly points towards the hypothesis of *resurrection*. The normal growth pattern of our personality calls not only for our leaving the material body, but also for our *assuming a spiritualized body*. To quote once more the analogy of birth and weaning, the crisis is absolutely necessary for us if we are to break out of environments that have become too narrow for us, but the change will be beneficial only if the subject, now no longer under compulsion, reconquers in complete freedom the relationships that hitherto were imposed upon him. A child does free himself from his mother in the biological sense. But while the freedom thus acquired makes it possible for the child to break every relationship with his mother, it also enables him to achieve an intimate, deep, personal union. Instinct must yield its place to love. The right kind of evolution is undoubtedly the one that carries the child toward an adult reconquest of filial affection, instead of pushing him into isolated selfishness. No rupture has an intrinsic, definitive value. The human being is born into a home that was built before his arrival; later he established another home wherein he himself carries the burden of responsibility. Before he may become a teacher, he must be a student. The same change comes about in every other field. Should we not suppose, therefore, that the person himself will finally reverse the direction of his relationship with the body, not in order to break all the ties, but to get away from the present body as it is imposed, passive, material fact, and recreate a new body as a substance completely subjected to the spirit?

Resurrection seems to be part of the normal curve of our destiny. Since I am by nature an incarnate spirit, I shall again acquire a body, but it will be fashioned according to my own will. If I like my earthly body as it is, I shall be free to assume a new body exactly like it. But whether alike or different, this new one is truly *mine*: one that I actively will.

Second Aspect: *Widening of the Environment*

My relationship with the body is the center and symbol of all the relationships that make up my being. At the moment of death, each value will become questionable in a much more radical manner than at the time of the teenage crisis. Once more I shall have to take a deliberate stand concerning the universe, my fellow creatures, myself, and God. But since this time the choice is an irrevocable one, I obviously need an infinitely better knowledge of everything than I could ever expect to acquire on earth. This exigency is also inscribed in the trend of my spiritual growth.

Of course, many will raise the objection: "Spiritual activity is impossible without the concomitant activity of the brain." Let us suppose that this statement is shown elsewhere to be true, as far as earthly becoming is concerned. But if this becoming is essentially a transitional process, we have no right to transpose its specific law into the hereafter. An embryo receives the oxygen it needs through the cord. The latter is absolutely required, but only for a certain time. On birth, a child leaves his mother's womb: the cord is broken. But the baby breathes now through his lungs. Is not the relationship between the present body and the spiritual person something analogous to the relationship between the embryo and the motherly placenta? Does not this present body, this indispensable but temporary abode which is mine while the *becoming* lasts, represent in a way the mould wherein the *being* I am to become is cast? As far as the brain is concerned, it is the organ of attention, enabling the person to integrate himself into biological becoming. It is not, however, a condition of the very being of the person. When the latter—precisely at the moment of death—is delivered from life and becoming, the function of the brain is eliminated (like that of the cord at the moment of birth), while spiritual activity goes on unhampered. The spirit, in fact, will at last be able to come out into its own according to its fundamental ordination toward universality.

For a person, death is far from being the escape route from this world; rather, it marks the beginning of a deeper kind of union. When the umbilical cord breaks at the moment of birth, a new, vast horizon opens out. It will continue to extend. The earthly body, this placenta of the spiritual person, is a nourishing as well as a restrictive agent. It will be abandoned in so far as it means limitation; as a result of this, the person will find that his relationship with the world becomes easier and really universal. Death enlarges our "situation" indefinitely.

Third Aspect: Deepening of Consciousness

As knowledge is extended, consciousness deepens. Our body is for us a condition of earthly existence and of personal ripening, but it also overshadows the light of the mind. Total reflection, which we have already been practicing, never achieves in this life the perfect intuition of the self. We find here again the analogy existing between the two kinds of birth. The organs of respiration are being prepared long before the baby utters his first cry. As the body must leave the maternal womb to carry out its own biological functions, so also a person must leave the material body if he is to carry out fully his proper activities.

Grasping his own self to the very depths, the human being will then discover all of his constitutive relationships with the world, with other men and especially with God as Creator and Final End. The wealth of his new knowledge and consciousness makes him capable of acting perfectly freely and everything depends thereupon.

Fourth Aspect: Radical Freedom

To the extent that personal life grows in me, I already become upon this earth a master of the relationships that constitute my being. I am powerless to modify the *proper* existence of the various realities. But it depends on me whether God is a person real *for me,* or practically inexistent; for I may live either as a God-loving person or as an atheist. It depends on me whether my fellow men are my brethren, or complete strangers to me; for I may either join them in the adventure of life, or decide to play my own solitary, disdainful little game. It depends on me whether the whole world makes wonderful sense by serving the cause of my divinization, or appears to me as absurd, revolting and hopeless; for I may either join the world in enthusiastic offering and joyful service, or break every relationship with it that goes beyond cold technique or selfish pleasure. It depends on me whether I achieve a sincere, loving, creative personality, or dry up in barren lucidity and malevolent destructiveness; for I may either return to my sources by fruitful recollection, or waste myself in introspection and pleasure seeking.

But it must be recognized that while on this earth I can only map out the direction of the movement; *I become* free, but *I am not* free yet in the full sense of the word. Freedom means that I am capable of establishing myself and determining personally my own manner of acting, or rather, my manner of being. We have seen that man achieves a progressive independence of the various forms of hereditary, familial, and social determinism, whether by accepting or fighting them; he does his best to find his way among a host of obscure forces and attempts—if he truly cares to become free—to draw from them the best advantage for his personal ends. But every earthly choice offered to this precarious freedom seems nothing but preliminary practice or "rehearsal" for a future, final option; it helps train and prepare my freedom for birth. Let us apply once more the analogy of biological birth to the realm of the spirit. An embryo goes through almost all the acts it will have to perform after it is born; the heart finds its proper rhythm; the unborn baby moves his head, arms and legs; he even absorbs and digests in some small measure. In the same manner, we train ourselves in this stage of becoming for our future birth to life everlasting; and this regardless of the length of our earthly history and its circumstances.

There is hardly any common measure between this progressive initiation and the sudden revelation that will consummate it at the moment of death. If the child could remember, he would tell us how deep the chasm is that separates his life in the womb from the existence upon which he has been cast by birth, and how prenatal life, while being a preparation of what was to follow, has revealed nothing concerning life in the open world. Does not our life on earth represent, in relation to our *being,* what prenatal existence represented in relation to our *becoming?* "In dying," says Franklin, "we consummate our birth." The old Martyrologies have a wonderful name for death: *dies natalis,* the day of true birth when I shall fashion my own self to be what I desire to be everlastingly. The Platonic saying, "Life is an apprenticeship to death," acquires in this setting a new, profound meaning. The all-important act of our earthly life is its very last act, whereby *becoming* yields its place to *being*. It is the act of death.

Yes, death is an act, in our hypothesis. The man who witnesses the dying of another one is rather inclined to see nothing but passivity and weakness. The reason is that he notices only the decline of becoming, the failure of this temporal body which, in fact, begins to decay when it has fulfilled its role. This saddening sight, however, is only the reverse of reality. When my being breaks the chains of subjection to the world of determinism and constraint, it is able finally to blossom out in full, and chooses the relationships that will constitute it in the future. At that moment I shall know in perfect clearness the reality of God, of my fellow humans, of the world, and of myself—a reality my freedom is powerless either to destroy or to create. What I have to create is *their reality for me;* my being-with-them or my being-without-them; for I may either accept these relationships with grateful love, or reject them with self-centered, proud egotism. It will depend on me whether the final outcome is communion or isolation, friendship or hatred; and what is really important for me, my *being* (as distinguished from my *existence*), will be defined precisely by the final stand I shall have freely taken up.

With or *without*: everything hinges upon this alternative. Each of our free acts is really a choice between the two directions which these conjunctions imply.

At the moment of death the human *being* takes his own measure. The attitude, the orientation he prefers to take will be his for all eternity. That is the full meaning of the aphorism: "All men are equal in the sight of death." At this final moment, the only thing that counts is the fundamental orientation of the person toward communion or isolation. Every man, whatever his social status, family background, or other existential conditions may have been, will have adopted this orientation step by step, but by personal choices.

A man who all his life has been orientated toward love, seeking an ever more profound union with God and his neighbor, will blossom out in all spontaneity when full communion is finally open to him. As for the self-centered man, he is mainly the one for whom the final option is a tragic instant. Of course, he may still change completely as he steps upon the platform where he is to stay for ever. But his long-acquired habits make a reversal all the more difficult as selfishness has taken such deep roots. Although the option is offered to him in an entirely new context, it is quite possible, after all, that the finite and proud being should cling rigidly to its refusal of love, and prefer to remain for ever alone.

The theory of final option at the moment of death is neither "proved" nor "revealed"; it is an hypothesis. In our opinion, it is well supported in philosophy and in theology; but we have no time here to develop the arguments which strengthen it. In the sense of this essay, we have now come to the point of winding up.

The meaning of the earthly adventure is to train the spiritual person for that free act whereby he is to establish his own being. Man is an incarnated spirit who is in the act of *becoming* before he attains the fullness of his *being*. He is the flower and crown of a universe, itself evolutionary, where, in a stage-to-stage process, the same great law of concentration and synthesis prevails, which in the case of man calls for inner unification and communion of love. The whole material creation is nothing but a womb, pregnant with the human mind, an immense parable rich in meaning. God Himself made it to be such, that it might serve to train our free will which, one day, will respond to the invitation of His Love. A universe in the making, a personality still in the period of formation, contains nothing that can be fixed at once: even errors and faults may be turned to good if, at the end of the becoming, a last act sums up this experience into a definitive option.

In the last page of André Malraux's *La Condition Humaine,* old Gisors says: "You know the saying: it takes nine months to bring a man to life, but only one instant to kill him. . . . Listen: it takes not nine months, but sixty years to make a man, sixty years of sacrifice, of acts of will . . . of so many things! and when man is finally made, when nothing childish, nothing adolescent remains in him, when he is really and truly a man, he is no longer good for anything but dying."

A bitter statement, no doubt, that sums up the whole book and expresses the hopeless philosophy its author stood for at the time. "Life is absurd; everything is destroyed at death." But the same statement could be interpreted in a different light. Yes, when a man has truly become a man, he is no longer good for anything but death, for his whole growth had no other purpose; for death is the process, the crossing, whereby life is finally able to blossom out in full. No, nine months are not enough to make a man. The first pregnancy prepares him only for bodily birth. It is the second pregnancy—the time allotted to him in this world —that prepares him for spiritual birth. The first birth destines him for death; only the second makes him enter life. "We are born to die, but we die to live." Death is man's true birth: his birth to life everlasting.

Chapter Thirteen

RESURRECTION AS HOPE

JÜRGEN MOLTMANN

How can one identify with one's bodily life, seeing that one must expect bodily death and that one experiences it daily in suffering and disappointments? And yet we also must ask conversely: How can one live at all, if one does not identify with one's transient and mortal being? Either one must accept death as belonging to life, or one must renounce this life from the start. In this respect life and death cannot be harmonized in human existence.

Apparently the Christian faith, precisely in the midst of suffering that appears whenever finite life is expected to be the locale of infinite bliss, evolved the resurrection hope. In other words, the love in which we fully identify ourselves with this transient, vulnerable, and mortal life and the resurrection hope belong together and interpret each other. The Christian resurrection hope does not deny the importance of our earthly life by making us dream of heaven. If rightly understood, it makes us ready to accept our mortal life and completely to identify it. This hope does not differentiate between body and soul like the Greek concept of immortality, but makes us ready to animate the mortal body and thus also to humanize the repressive society of having.

The resurrection hope is thus not an "opium of the beyond," but a "power of worldly life." The resurrection hope claims paradoxically: *Caro est cardo salutis* (Tertullian).[1]

Probably from the mouth of Jesus himself we received that strange eschatological principle of life: "He who finds his life will lose it, and he who loses his life for my sake will find it" (Mk 8:35). We often rediscover this thought in a secularized form. "If you don't risk your life, ne'er will you win it," said Friedrich Schiller. And Hegel wrote: "Not the life that shuns death and keeps itself pure from destruction, but the life that bears death and keeps itself in death, is the life of the spirit."[2] In the modern "society of having" and in the institutional escapes from the battle of life, boredom often raises its ugly head, since life appears meaningless and one no longer finds anything for which one could take a stand. Man, however, does not find identity in this life, in remaining isolated and in keeping his soul for himself, but only in going out of himself and becoming personally, socially, and politically incarnate.

Which hope is strong enough to make this incarnation and the identification and the commitment of one's life meaningful beyond all frustration, which finally means beyond death? Man always regains his identity from that to which he gives himself. If this is mortal and transient, he will die and perish himself. In the early church it was said that man finds himself again in eternity, if he gives himself to something eternal, namely, God. Today we perhaps should say that man finds himself again in the future, if he risks his life for a coming future that will not pass away. He will find himself again in the Kingdom of God, if he risks his life for the coming of this Kingdom, and if he takes his cross upon himself, as the Word of God would have him do. The resurrection hope readies one for a life in love without reservation. Therefore we can say conversely that creative and self-giving love mirrors future resurrection under the

---

1. Tertullian, **De resurrectione mortuorum,** 8, 2.
2. Cf. G. W. F. Hegel, **Phenomenology of the Mind,** trans. James Baillie, London, George Allen and Unwin, 1910, p. 93.

conditions of this present life. The resurrection into life and freedom is here anticipated in the reverse movement of the incarnation, of self-oblation and faithful labor. Love, creating new life out of nothing, is resurrection in this life. Not the *corpse* that we can dissect objectively, but the *body* with which we identify in love, stands in the horizon of the resurrection hope. There is no meaningful hope for the body we *have,* but only for the body we *are.* In love we break through the deadly category of having and arrive at the category of affirmed being. Herein alone lies resurrection hope in accord with the Christian faith. In this acceptance of the body and this identification of our self with the body we experience an anticipation of the final liberation and redemption of the body. The body is being liberated from the repressions of fear, as it is liberated from the law and the repressions of the law. It enters into the sphere of influence of the gospel and of the freedom of faith.

This "prolepsis" of the resurrection of the body has psychological implications. I am thinking, for example, of the book by N. O. Brown, *Life against Death.*[3] But it also has sociopolitical consequences. What did Moses Hess and Karl Marx want in their earlier writings? They wanted to break the domination of the category of having over the category of being and they looked for social conditions in which the inhuman and artificial world of things, goods, and money is replaced by a world of true humanity, in which one can "exchange love for love only, and friendship for friendship only," but cannot buy either one or capitalize on both.[4] Of course, such a world of true humanity is a dream. Man is obviously subjected to both having and being, and cannot manage to live in fealty to one category only. But he must search in each situation for a meaningful and live balance between the two. Man always *is* body, but simultaneously he *has* this body as his very own. He must be able to identify with the

---

3. N. O. Brown, **Life Against Death: The Psychological Meaning of History,** Middletown, Conn., Wesleyan University Press, 1959.
4. Karl Marx, **Die Frühschriften,** ed. S. Landshut, Stuttgart, Alfred Kröner Verlag, 1964, p. 301.

reality of his life, and yet at the same time to transcend it and reflect on it. Spontaneity and reflection both belong to man's very being. And yet one will have to look in the *culture of reflection* in the modern world for the necessary humanization of a new personal spontaneity and a satisfactory social identification. Dietrich Bonhoeffer thus emphasized the passionate "worldliness of the Christian faith," for which the "knowledge of death and resurrection are ever present."[5] For this reason there are also many who today in the resurrection hope find the power for social and political revolt against a world of death, fear, repression, and alienation. In the *anastasis* is contained the *stasis,* and in the resurrection, the revolution. Jesus' resurrection can be understood as the protest of life against death, and the life in the spirit of the resurrection pertains to the "making alive of the dead conditions" (Hegel) and the humanization of the human condition as a whole.[6]

This makes for a change in the ancient and troublesome *theodicy* question. Nature with its orders and its chaos does not give an answer. History, this "mishmash of error and brute force," in Goethe's terminology, does not give an answer either. The theodicy question must become a questioning of the future, and from the future we can expect the advent of a new creation of God, and in this expectation we can actively try to change the present, so that our world becomes transformed into the recognizable world of God, and our sinful humanity into the recognizable humanity before God.

In a time when God was questioned, the Christian faith saw, in Jesus, God's incarnation. Not the resurrection, but the incarnation; not Easter, but Christmas stood at the center. In a time when man began to regard himself as questionable, faith saw in Jesus the true man, the creative archetype of the divine man. Today the future is becoming more and more the pressing ques-

---

5. D. Bonhoeffer, **Letters and Papers from Prison,** rev. ed. by E. Bethge, trans. R. H. Fuller, New York, Macmillan, 1962, pp. 225f.
6. Cf. W.-D. Marsch, **Gegenwart Christi in der Gesellschaft,** München: Chr. Kaiser Verlag, 1965.

tion for a mankind that is now able to destroy itself. Thus Christian faith discovers today in God the power of a future that stems itself against the destruction of the world. The God of the exodus and of the resurrection is the "God of hope" rather than the "God above" or the "ground of being." He is in history "the coming God," as the Old Testament prophets said, who announces his coming in his promises and his lowly Messiah. He is "the absolute future" (Karl Rahner) or, figuratively, the Lord of the future, who says, "Behold, I make all things new."

If we simultaneously begin to think of God and future, faith and hope, we move in a new way close to the primitive Christian Easter message. We are able to understand it again eschatologically. We can recognize in the inexplicable *novum* of Christ the anticipation and the incarnation of the ultimately or universally new, which in the coming of the recreating God can be hoped for. God is the power of the future. God is the power of the new. Jesus himself has been translated into the future of the new. He represents this future and at the same time mediates it. Following the emphasis on divine Sonship and the emphasis on true humanity, the old titles for Jesus, "Messiah" and *ho erchomenos*, the "coming one," seem quite timely again. In him, who from cross, God-forsakenness, and hell was raised, we become certain of a future which will conquer God-forsakenness and hell. But this is not everything: The fulfillment of the resurrection hope must now be joined with the expectation of a future which has not existed before, with the expectation of the presence of the God who announces himself in Word and Spirit. The ultimately new lies in the promise: "He will dwell with them, and they shall be his people" (Rev 21:3). The resurrection hope can fulfill itself only in the future of God in which God is really God and will be "all in all" (1 Cor 15:28).

The hope for such a presence of God can be fulfilled, however, only if the negatives of death, suffering, tears, guilt, and evil have disappeared from reality, that is, in a new creation, which, figuratively speaking, is no longer a mixture of day and night, earth and sea, and in which, ontologically speaking, being and nonbeing are no longer intertwined. The hope for the future, in which God is God and a new creation his dwelling place, the expectation of that home of identity in which man is at one with God, nature, and himself radically anew confronts the unfulfilled present with the theodicy question. Where freedom has come near, the chains begin to hurt. Where life is close, death becomes deadly. Where God proclaims his presence, the God-forsakenness of the world turns into suffering. Thus the theodicy question, born of suffering and pain, negatively mirrors the positive hope for God's future. We begin to suffer from the conditions of our world if we begin to love the world. And we begin to love the world if we are able to discover hope for it. And we discover hope for this world if we hear the promise of a future which stands against frustration, transiency, and death.

Chapter Fourteen

DEATH AND COSMIC RESURRECTION

BY KILIAN MCDONNELL, O.S.B.

There have been in antiquity those who looked upon death as a
good of a very high order. The soul was imprisoned in the body,
according to Plato, and it is always good to flee a prison. In this
view, death is a freeing of the soul from "this evil thing," the body.
Death is the great liberator.

Apart from some such philosophical theorists, there has been
an almost universal consternation on the part of man as he faces
the inevitability of death. The Greek philosophers looked upon
death with greater calm than did the Greek poets who protested
against it. Many, though meeting death with fortitude, looked
upon it as an indecent ravaging of life. To die was to tear madly
at meaning and purpose. Marcus Aurelius, who together with
Socrates surely belongs to the noblest figures of antiquity, had
only the deepest contempt for Christianity. One would rightly
expect that the death of the Christian martyrs would have moved
this Stoic to respect if not to admiration. Quite the contrary.
It was precisely the martyrs' death which he regarded with so
little sympathy. The alacrity with which the Christians met their
death, he looked upon as madness. The Stoic faced death dis-

passionately, steeled to face the inevitable with dignity and discipline; the Christian martyrs died singing hymns and canticles and in some cases in a kind of ecstasy. They died, not without fear, but joyously for the cause of Christ, because they knew that by so dying they stood within a powerful redemptive process.

Dylan Thomas has been accused of many things, but never of being a Stoic. Like the chaste-souled Roman, Marcus Aurelius, the not-so-chaste Welshman, Dylan Thomas, looked upon death as an unpardonable enormity. To his dying father Thomas wrote: "Do not go gentle into that night, old age should burn and rave at close of day. Rage, rage against the dying of the light."

Even the greater part of the Old Testament looked upon death as a curse, though it yearned for an immortality which embraced the whole man (cf. Is 38:18, 19; Is 26:19). The New Testament takes up this Old Testament expectation and asserts that immortality has to do not only with the whole man, but with the whole of creation. The immortality promised by the New Testament is explicitly opposed to the Greek concept of immortality as the soul set free from the prison of the body. The Christian "dies for the Lord" just as he has tried to live for him. From being an anguished necessity, death becomes an object of beatitude: "Blessed are they who die in the Lord! Let them henceforth rest from their labors!" (Acts 14:13).

Death in Christ

Central to the New Testament witness is the belief that by dying, Jesus Christ has conquered death. One could rightly ask the question, then, why those who have been "united with him" (Rom 6:5) and have been plunged into the death of Christ, should yet die. Further, the question can be asked why the New Testament writers would look upon death, not as a matter of minor importance, but as the last enemy still to be conquered. Though Christ has won the victory, that victory has not yet been manifested in its fullness, a manifestation which will take place in the person of Christ when he will return at the end of time. The victory which has already been won by Christ becomes ours by faith, by a Spirit-filled life, by the sacramental imitation (being baptized into Christ's death and resurrection and by "showing forth the death of Christ" in the Eucharist) and, lastly, by a physical death. By dying a physical death one dies "to the Lord" (Rom 14:8), that is, in our death his is repeated and fulfilled (cf. Jn 16:2; Rom 8:36ff; 1 Cor 15:31; 2 Cor 4:7ff; Col 1:24; 1 Pt 2:18ff; 1 Pt 3:13ff., etc.). The suffering of Christ, with its terrors and its peace, becomes ours through dying in Christ (cf. Mk 14:34ff; Mt 27:32-50; Mk 15:21-37; Lk 23: 26-49; Jn 19:17-30).

The participation of the dying Christian in the dying and death of Christ is decisive for an understanding of either the New Testament teaching or of the liturgy of dying. It is only through the participation of the dying Christian in the dying and death of Christ that the essential contradiction to the constitution of man as a composite being is taken away. It would not take away the essential contradiction if the participation in the Christ event stopped at the death of Christ. If we die with Christ and are buried with him and if that is where the process stops, then truly we of all men are the most to be pitied. To be united to the death of Christ is a great deal, but it is not enough. Through and because of the death of Christ we are united with his rising. There is an absolute dependence of futurity of either the body or soul on the resurrection of Christ. Without the resurrection, there is no hope of life for the whole composite being. Without the resurrection of Christ there is, in the Christian dispensation, no possibility, however remote, of personal existence after death. Without the resurrection, all talk of the life of man after death, or the life of the soul after death or the life of the body after death, breaks down. This is one of the reasons why the Paschal mystery is at the heart of Christian life and the liturgical life of the Church.

The resurrection is not, even in the biblical witness, simply a proof of Christ's divinity—if he could rise from the dead then, surely, he is divine. The resurrection event and the Easter cele- bration stand at the very core of any thought of the beyond, of futurity, of continuity on the other side of death, of a history which moves beyond death into a final consummation when Christ will lay the kingdom at the feet of the Father and all will be all in all. There is no possibility of relating eternity to the human dimension and to continued human existence in some form without the resurrection of Christ. Finitude of duration and the end of time is the lot of all men unless Christ has risen from the dead. Infinity beyond death is radically, irrevocably tied to the resurrection of Christ. I belabor the point because it must be clear that the resurrection of Christ is our only hope for personal existence beyond death, a point not generally understood.

One could possibly speculate on what God could have done; what other possible economies of salvation he could have instituted. One could posit the possibility of other conditions of personal existence which would not be dependent on the resurrection of Christ. But in the economy of salvation which has been revealed to us in Christ, these other ways and other conditions simply do not exist. Once again, without the resurrection of Christ there is no resurrection of the Christian, and without the resurrection of the Christian there is no possibility of personal existence, because personal existence within the human context is tied to bodily existence. The existence of the soul apart from the body is not personal existence in the full sense. Thus, for St. Thomas Aquinas, the soul separated from the body is not a "person" in the proper sense of the term. This is not to deny to the blessed in heaven a conscious and "personal" existence; rather, it is to insist that the full concept of "person" is tied to some form of bodily existence. One must not fall into the error of thinking that the soul is attached to the body by some casual relationship. The relation to the body is of the very texture of the soul. The soul apart from the body is in a highly unnatural condition, so unnatural that in this separated condition it cannot be considered a person in the full sense of person.

We have been using the terms body and soul very clumsily. In the Platonic tradition body and soul are opposed, and this is the manner in which most of us use the terms. But this is not the biblical way of thinking, except for some passages in Wisdom and a minor remnant in the New Testament. In Hebrew *the soul is the man,* so that one would not say that a man *has* a soul, but that he *is* a soul; nor would one say that a man *has* a body but that he *is* a body. Thus, man is described in Genesis as a "living soul" (Gen 2:7). The biblical intent is not to distinguish between body and soul, as in Plato, but between the Maker and the man he has made. As a matter of fact, there is no Hebrew word for body, only for corpse, flesh and meat.

Decision in Death

One of the most important developments in the theology of death in recent years is the ever increasing importance given to personal decision at the moment of death. If personal decision is a constitutive element of a Christian's death, then death cannot be merely something which is passively endured, as Karl Rahner says, "destruction coming upon us from without." Death must also be conceived as something which rises from the free act of the will, from within man.

There are two poles, or rather a series of poles, which determine the dynamics of death. This series of poles or opposites are reflections of the essentially dialectic nature of human existence. We are acted upon and we initiate action; we passively suffer and we actively achieve; events are forced upon us and we are the creators of events; the components of our conscious and physical life are set in disarray by forces from without, the components of our conscious and physical life are ordered from within by the forces of self-possession; we are creatures of necessity and freedom. We are creatures of constraint, vulnerability and necessity. We are vulnerable because we are sons of Adam. By the fall of Adam, the first father of the human race, sin entered the world, and through sin, death (Rom 5:12 and 17; 1 Cor 15:21). Since that time, all men are under the constraint to die in Adam, so that St. Paul can say that death rules the world (Rom 5:14). The wages of sin is death and the universality of sin is the sign of the universality of death. I use the word "sign" advisedly.

One should not press the relationship between sin and death. It does not seem that Adam would have lived forever in his then present condition if he had not sinned. (Here enters the whole question of the paradisal state which is being discussed again today.) Rather than postulate a state of supernatural and preternatural perfection, which one would expect at the end of a development rather than at the beginning, there is a tendency to think of man as mortal even before sin, mortal in the sense in which we experience our mortality. Or if one would opt for an ideal paradisal state in which there was no death as we experience it, it may be that man would have undergone a painless, indeed glorious, transformation and transfiguration after a period of terrestrial life, which transformation would be a type of death. In either case, death is the wages of sin somewhat in the same manner that man must work by the sweat of his brow and the earth will bring forth thorns and thistles because of Adam's sin. Neither work nor death are radically excluded from Adam's life before sin; but both take on an entirely different character after Adam's fall. And the modality of work and death after the fall are signs of the presence and the reign of sin.

Because man is under sin and therefore under constraint, he is not free to choose the moment of his death. Death comes like the thief in the night, when one least expects it, when one is taking his ease, saying: "Soul, you have plenty of good things laid by for many years to come; take it easy, eat, drink and have a good time" (Lk 12:16-21). The necessity of death makes us vulnerable; the uncertainty of its moment makes our vulnerability manifest.

Our theologizing should not divorce itself entirely from the human dimension. And even the assurances of a future life and the resurrection of man and a life of unending beatitude with God should not close our minds to death as an end to a good of a very high order: terrestrial existence. Death then marks the end to a mode of existence which we have up to this point called home and family and occupation. In this regard death is a violence done to our concrete situation, an emptying of historical existence as we know it. We face death blindly and we may trip over it at any moment.

But we are in Christ and the death we die is not the Adam-death but the Christ-death. Therefore, at the same time that we are vulnerable, under constraint and necessity, we are free. We still die in fear (to escape all possibility of fear would be to escape the human condition) but we can freely choose the death we are under constraint to die. In death we have the opportunity to reach out freely to the judgment of God and to embrace willingly, freely, lovingly that which he as our Father has decreed. At the moment of death, when we wake to the full consciousness, we choose this moment, and none other, to go beyond the pale of living. This is not simply an event forced on us from without, but an event chosen from within; death becomes an object of a free and deliberate consent, a deed of a man dying in Christ. This moment, which is the unmeasured point between full life and a complete death, is the point at which man will make an act of knowing and choosing, when the mind is free of its material principle, the brain. At this moment the mind can possess itself within itself without acting through sense knowledge and the sense world. It can freely open itself to that infinity of which it is capable, an infinity which is implicit in the definition of man. In this view the end of man has its definitive character as something chosen.

The free choice made at this point is more than a choice of death over life, it is a choice in regard to God. The free embrace of God's judgment is a choice for God himself. Though salvation is a free, unmerited gift, initiated by God and brought to completion by God, man must take a stance with regard to God at the moment of death. Death is not just the occasion on which God decides irrevocably the final destiny of man; it is also the occasion when man makes his irrevocable choice with regard to God. The destiny of man involves more than man being acted upon, man being the passive receiver. Man has to act with regard to his destiny; it, too, is a matter of choice. And God is a matter of free choice.

Cosmic Resurrection

To choose God is to choose a resurrection to life, to participate in the triumph of Christ over the last enemy, death. It would
be to truncate the whole mystery of redemption were one to
spiritualize salvation and think of the final reality as a matter
of the soul. We do not, as a matter of fact, save our souls. Nor
does God. God is not interested in our souls; he is interested in
man, just as we see and experience him, body and soul. But God
wants to save more than man; he wants to save man's world.
The nature of salvation goes beyond man and includes the rivers,
trees, fields, flowers, mountains, moon, sun, and stars, the whole
of the created universe. This and nothing less is what salvation
is about.

We do not know in any great detail about the salvation of
the whole universe. We do not know, simply because God has
not chosen to tell us very much. But this much we do know: the
world as we now know it will die and be destroyed, just as
we die and our terrestrial existence as we now know it will go
down in death and decay. But just as the body will rise and be
transformed in Christ, transfigured in Christ, so will the created
universe rise in Christ and be transformed in Christ, transfigured
in Christ.

That the created universe should partake of the glory of the
risen Christ should not be a matter of surprise. If Christ is the
head of all creation and if the whole universe was created in him,
through him and for him, and if he holds all things in unity,
then the resurrection of Christ and of man should rightly demand
the resurrection and transfiguration of the universe. Paul gives
the theological presupposition to this doctrine in Colossians 1:15-
18: "He is the image of the unseen God and the first-born of all
creation, for in him were created all things in heaven and on
earth: everything visible and everything invisible . . . all things
were created through him and for him. Before anything was created,
he existed, and he holds all things in unity."

The Vision of Paul

The vision of Paul embraces the whole universe in a trans-temporal leap which spans the past, present and future; a leap which relates the inner core of created matter and its history to the pre-existent Christ so far as this Christ has become an historical person. The relationship of Christ to the whole of creation is not that external relationship which exists between a model and that which is made in the image of the model. The dependence is ontological. One cannot understand the nature and destiny of the created universe unless one understands the nature and destiny of Christ. The created universe is intelligible only through the Christ on which it is ontologically dependent.

In Ephesians, St. Paul speaks of the redemptive plan of God as the recapitulation of all things in Christ: "He has let us know the mystery of his purpose . . . that he would bring everything together under Christ, as head, everything in the heavens and everything on earth" (1:8-10). And finally he speaks of the cosmic rebirth in Christ which is developed in the context of Christ's resurrection. "How infinitely great is the power that he [the Father] has exercised for us believers. This you can tell from the strength of his power at work in Christ, when he used it to raise him from the dead and to make him sit at his right hand in heaven. . . . He has put all things under his feet, and made him, as the ruler of everything, the head of the Church; which is his body, the fullness of him who fills the whole creation" (1:19-23). As Stanislaus Lyonnet, to whom this section is indebted, has said: "God has created nothing for death, but rather only for life." If the final destiny of Christ is resurrection and glorification, then the final destiny of man must be resurrection and glorification, and with him the whole of the created universe which is his proper bodily context. A body apart from the universe is a great anomaly.

The text most frequently quoted in regard to cosmological redemption is Romans 8:18-22. "I consider that the sufferings of the present time are not worthy to be compared with the glory which will be revealed. For with eager longing creation awaits the revelation of the sons of God. . . . For creation itself also will be delivered from its slavery to corruption into the freedom of the glory of the sons of God. For we know that all creation groans in the pains of childbirth until today."

It must be admitted that the meaning of this text is disputed. A great part of the dispute hangs on the meaning of the Greek word for "creation" in the text. Some of the Fathers (Irenaeus, Methodius, Gregory Nazianzus, Chrysostom, Cyril of Alexandria, Tertullian) thought that the word "creation" meant all the creation visible to man; others (Clement of Alexandria, Origen, Hilary) thought it meant all rational creation (men and angels); while others (Theodoret, Ambrose, Thomas Aquinas) took a radical cosmological view, holding that it meant the whole of the created universe. St. Ambrose wrote: "In him (Christ) the world rose; in him the heavens rose; in him the earth rose: there will be a new heavens and a new earth." St. Thomas is even more explicit: "Because all corporal beings exist in some way for man, it is fitting that at that time (after the last judgment) the state of the entire corporal universe will be transformed, so that it may be in harmony with what will then be the state of man. And since men will then be incorruptible, the present state of corruptibility will be removed from the corporal universe. This is what the Apostle teaches (Rom 8:21). Thus, since men will not only be freed from corruption, but clothed in glory, the material universe must also acquire in its way a certain light of glory." Some important contemporary exegetes uphold this interpretation, including Lyonnet, Lagrange, Viard, Schmidt and Kuss.

One should be very careful in quoting texts which use apocalyptic language, but there are exegetes (Chaine, Lenski) who relate to the universal transformation the passage from 2 Peter 3:13: "We look for a new heavens and a new earth according to his promises." And finally, Apocalypse 21:5 has been given a cosmological exegesis (Caird). St. John writes of the majestic voice of God calling out to the whole of creation from the throne of glory: "Behold, I make all things new!" It is clear that cosmic transformation is nothing other than the bold framework in which the individual and corporate transformation takes place. No salvation is complete if the terrestrial dimension of humanity is disregarded. In the risen universe, individual and collective salvation is perfected.

The close relationship Paul envisages between creation and Christ on the one hand, and the resurrection of man and the resurrection of Christ on the other, makes it possible for us to give personal, corporate and cosmic meaning to death. If pressed to summarize the meaning of death in one short phrase—and it must be admitted that every attempt is a truncation—one could say that the meaning of death is resurrection; personal, corporate and cosmic resurrection.

EPILOG

HEAVEN: THE ESSENCE OF OUR FUTURE

LADISLAUS BOROS

What do we arrive at if we project our deepest experience of the life and vitality of the world into heaven? We think of a world of full growth and expansion, lived in God's company, integrating the whole process of evolution, all life and feeling that exists in the world—from inorganic matter through organisms to spirit—into the infinite happiness of God.

Revelation adds one image after another to suggest to us plainly and simply a boundless happiness eternally bestowed: I shall be a God to him, and he shall be my child; the just will sit with Christ on the throne of God; they will judge the world, they will shine like the sun; God will give them the morning star. These are all images of happiness, purity, clarity, and vitality; intelligible to the simplest, and yet by their profound symbolism they transcend everything that can be expressed. What theologian has yet fully drawn out the wealth contained in these metaphors of sitting on God's throne, judging the world, being sun and light, bearing a crown of glory, possessing the morning star?

What does Christ promise? To a Samaritan woman, water; to the people, bread; to fishermen, nets filled to overflowing; to merchants, precious pearls; to the farm-worker that his hoe will one day unexpectedly unearth a treasure; to the peasants, an abundant harvest; to us all, knowledge and security. The Book of Revelation is radiant with all the colors in the world; precious stones gleam; the voices of nature accompany men's songs of triumph; the air is filled with perfumes rising from golden vessels. He who is true and faithful comes on a white horse accompanied by squadrons of horsemen. His name is Word of God, King of Kings. His mantle is soaked in blood. In a final battle he saved our nature for fulfillment. He is celebrating the marriage feast of the Lamb. A voice rings out from heaven: "He who conquers, I will make him a pillar in the temple of my God; ever shall he go out of it." To be a pillar in God's temple means to be continually active, to bear up the world, secure and serene, in the eternal vitality of unending personal life.

Jesus repeatedly describes eternal life as union with God. "If a man loves me, he will keep my word, and my Father will love him, and we will come to him and make our home with him." "You will eat and drink at my table in my kingdom." "Behold, I stand at the door and knock; if any one hears my voice and opens the door, I will come in to him and eat with him, and he with me. He who conquers, I will grant him to sit with me on my throne, as I myself conquered and sat down with my Father on his throne." God becomes my beloved, forever.

Let us now try to forget the words and catch some glimpse of the mysterious import of Christ's prayer at the Last Supper: "Father, the world has not known thee, but I have known thee; and these know that thou hast sent me. I made known to them thy name, and I will make it known, that the love with which thou hast loved me may be in them and I in them."

This love of God in us will unfold in heaven into an eternal reality. One hardly dares try to express what that means in growing intensity of being and radiant personal life. It is ultimately of little importance whether we are immortal by nature, or in what form the world will awaken in us to the new being of the resurrection. We love God; God loves us. His love is infinite and embraces all that is. That love will become our own being, experienced, accomplished, and eternal.

Christ's resurrection has inaugurated the last days. To remain true to our vocation to love God, we must live here and now as though we were already in heaven. That is our destiny and our mission. Under various names God incarnate promised us life: kingdom of heaven, land of the living, perfect consolation, fulfillment of our desires, boundless mercy, the company of God. He also pointed out our way to this: detachment from self, gentleness, peacemaking, hunger and thirst for "righteousness." All these are essential characteristics of the love by which man receives himself by giving himself.

SELECTED BIBLIOGRAPHY

Becqué, Maurice and Louis, **Life After Death** (New York: Haw-thorn Books, 1960).

Benoit, Pierre and Roland Murphy, eds., **Immortality and Resur-rection** [Concilium, Vol. 60] (New York: Herder & Herder, Inc., 1970).

Boros, Ladislaus, **The Mystery of Death** (New York: Herder & Herder, Inc., 1965).

————, **Pain and Providence** (Baltimore: Helicon Press, Inc., 1966).

————, **We Are Hope** (New York: Herder & Herder, Inc., 1970).

Bowker, John, **The Problem of Suffering in the Religions of the World** (New York: Cambridge University Press, 1970).

Brandon, S.G.F., **Judgment of the Dead** (New York: Charles Scribner's Sons, 1967).

Buber, Martin, **Good and Evil.** (New York: Charles Scribner's Sons, 1953).

Bultmann, Rudolph, **Life and Death** (London: A. and C. Black, 1965).

Cargas, Harry and Ann White, eds., **Death and Hope** (New York: Corpus Books, 1970).

Choron, Jacques, **Death and Western Thought** (New York: Collier Books, 1963).

Cobb, John, **God and the World** (Philadelphia: Westminster Press, 1965).

Continuum (1967), Vol. 5, No. 3, Autumn. Most of the issue is de-voted to the subject of Death.

Demske, James, **Being, Man and Death: A Key to Heidegger** (Lexington, Kentucky: University Press of Kentucky, 1970).

Evely, Louis, **Suffering** (New York: Herder & Herder, Inc., 1967).

Farrer, Austin, **Love Almighty and Ills Unlimited** (New York: Doubleday & Co., Inc., 1961).

Feifel, Herman, ed., **The Meaning of Death** (New York: McGraw-Hill, 1959).

Fitch, Robert, **Of Love and Suffering** (Philadelphia: Westminster Press, 1970).

Gatch, Milton, **Death: Meaning and Morality in Christian Thought** (New York: Seabury Press, 1969).

Gleason, Robert, **The World to Come** (New York: Sheed & Ward, 1958).

Godin, A., ed., **Death and Presence** (Brussels: Lumen Vitae Press, 1971).

Guardini, Romano, **The Last Things** (South Bend, Ind.: University of Notre Dame Press, 1966).

Heidegger, Martin, **Being and Time** (New York: Harper & Row, 1962).

Hick, John, **Evil and the God of Love** (New York: Harper and Row: 1966).

Journet, Charles, **The Meaning of Evil** (New York: Kenedy, 1963).

Kubler-Ross, Elizabeth, **On Death and Dying** (New York: The Macmillan Co., 1970).

Lepp, Ignace, **Death and Its Mysteries** (New York: The Macmillan Co., 1968).

Lewis, C.S., **The Problem of Pain** (New York: The Macmillan Co., 1944).

Madden, Edward and Peter Hare, **Evil and the Concept of God** (Springfield, Ill.: C. C. Thomas, 1968).

Marcel, Gabriel, **Presence and Immortality** (Pittsburgh: Duquesne University Press, 1967).

Maritain, Jacques, **God and the Permission of Evil** (Milwaukee: Bruce, 1966).

Mauriac, François, **Anguish and Joy of the Christian Life** (Wilkes-Barre, Pa.: Dimension Books, 1964).

Moltmann, Jürgen, **Theology of Hope** (New York: Harper & Row, 1967).

Mooney, Christopher, **Teilhard de Chardin and the Mystery of Christ** (New York: Harper & Row, 1965).

Mouroux, Jean, **The Mystery of Time** (New York: Desclee, 1964).

Murray, John C., **Problem of God** (New Haven: Yale University Press, 1964).

Nogar, Raymond, **The Lord of the Absurd** (New York: Herder & Herder, Inc., 1966).

Nowell, Robert, **What a Modern Catholic Believes about Death** (Chicago: Thomas More Press, 1972).

Ochs, Robert, **The Death in Every Now** (New York: Sheed & Ward, 1969).

Oraison, Marc, **Death and Then What?** (Paramus, N. J.: Newman Press, 1969).

Outler, Albert, **Who Trusts in God** (New York: Oxford University Press, 1968).

Padovano, Anthony, **Dawn Without Darkness** (Paramus, N. J.: Paulist Press, 1971).

Pieper, Josef, **Death and Immortality** (New York: Herder & Herder, Inc., 1969).

Rahner, Karl, **On the Theology of Death** (New York: Herder & Herder, Inc., 1961).

————, **Theological Investigations,** Vols. 2 and 4 (Baltimore: Helicon Press, Inc., 1966).

Ricoeur, Paul, **The Symbolism of Evil** (New York: Harper & Row, 1967).

Schillebeeckx, Edward and Boniface Willems, eds., **The Problem of Eschatology** [Concilium, Vol. 41] (Paramus, N. J.: Paulist Press, 1969).

Simpson, Michael, **Death and Eternal Life** (Notre Dame, Ind.: Fides Publishers, Inc., 1970).

Siwek, Paul, **The Philosophy of Evil** (New York: Ronald Press, 1951).

Sontag, Frederick, **God, Why did you do that?** (Philadelphia: Westminster Press, 1970).

Teilhard de Chardin, Pierre, **Christianity and Evolution** (New York: Harcourt, Brace, Jovanovich, 1971).

————, **The Divine Milieu** (New York: Harper & Row, 1960).

————, **The Phenomenon of Man** (New York: Harper & Row, 1959).

Thielicke, Helmut, **Death and Life** (Philadelphia: Fortress Press, 1970).

Tillich, Paul, **The Eternal Now** (New York: Charles Scribner's Sons, 1963).

————, **Systematic Theology,** Vol. 3, chs. 40-42 (Chicago: University of Chicago Press, 1963).

Troisfontaines, Roger, **I Do Not Die** (New York: Desclee, 1963).

Winklhofer, Alois, **The Coming of His Kingdom** (New York: Herder & Herder, Inc., 1963).

Wright, John, "The Theology of Death," pp. 687-695, **The New Catholic Encyclopedia,** Vol. 4 (New York: McGraw-Hill, 1967).

CONTRIBUTORS

ALBERT C. OUTLER, a renowned Methodist scholar, is professor of historical theology at Southern Methodist University and past president of the American Theological Society. Dr. Outler has traveled and lectured widely on ecumenical topics and is the author of **The Christian Tradition and the Unity We Seek, Who Trusts in God,** and editor of **John Wesley,** a volume in the Library of Protestant Thought.

JOHN HICK has received academic degrees from both Oxford and Cambridge Universities. Formerly a lecturer in the philosophy of religion at Cambridge University, he is presently professor of theology at the University of Birmingham in England. He is author of several books, including **Faith and Knowledge, Philosophy of Religion,** and **Evil and the God of Love.**

JOHN L. McKENZIE, a scripture scholar of international reputation, has taught at Notre Dame University and is presently professor of theology at DePaul University in Chicago. A popular lecturer and visiting professor, he is a prolific writer. His publications include **The Two-Edged Sword, Myths and Realities, The Power and the Wisdom, The Dictionary of the Bible,** and **Authority in the Church.**

JOSEPH BLENKINSOPP teaches at the University of Notre Dame in South Bend, Indiana. He holds a licentiate in scripture from the Pontifical Institute in Rome and a doctorate in theology from Oxford University. He has taught and lectured widely in both Great Britain and the United States. A frequent contributor to theological journals, he has also published several books, among them **Sketchbook of Biblical Theology, Celibacy, Ministry, Church, and Sexuality and the Christian Tradition.**

CHRISTOPHER F. MOONEY, S.J. is president of the Jesuit Woodstock College in New York City. He received his doctorate in theology from the Catholic Institute of Paris and has taught theology at St. Peter's, Canisius College, and Fordham University. The recipient of the National Catholic Book Award for 1966, he is the author of **Teilhard de Chardin and the Mystery of Christ, The Making of Man—Essays in the Christian Spirit, Prayer: The Problem of Dialogue with God,** and **The Presence and Absence of God.**

FRANÇOIS -H. LEPARGNEUR, O.P. is a professor in the department of anthropology at the **Universidade Federal de Minas Gerais,** Brazil. He is the author of many articles on philosophy and theology.

RAYMOND J. NOGAR, O.P. was a popular teacher and lecturer on college campuses in the United States. Father Nogar taught theology at Notre Dame College in Bellmont, California until his death in 1968. He is the author of **Science in Synthesis, The Wisdom of Evolution,** and **The Lord of the Absurd.**

LEONARD JOHNSTON was educated at Ushaw College in Durham, England. He studied theology and oriental languages at the University of Louvain and holds a licentiate in sacred scripture from the Biblical Institute in Rome. He taught biblical studies at Ushaw College and is now head of the divinity department at Mary Ward College of Education, Keyworth-Nottingham, England. He is a frequent contributor of articles to theological journals.

GEORGE J. DYER holds an S.T.L. and S.T.D. degree from St. Mary of the Lake Seminary, Mundelein, Illinois, where he is presently the Dean of Studies in the School of Theology. He is the editor of **Chicago Studies.** His published books include **Limbo: Unsettled Question, Sharing Responsibility in the Local Church,** and **Future Forms of Ministry.**

ROBERT J. OCHS, S.J. holds a theological degree from Innsbruck and an S.T.D. from the Catholic Institute of Paris. He is presently a professor of theology at the Bellarmine School of Theology in Chicago. A Fulbright Scholar, he is the author of **The Death in Every Now,** and **God is More Present than You Think.**

LADISLAUS BOROS, S.J. studied in the Jesuit Scholasticates of Hungary, Austria, Italy, and France. He received his doctorate in philosophy at the University of Munich. He is presently director of the course for the philosophy of religion at the University of Innsbruck. His published books include **The Mystery of Death, Pain and Providence, Meeting God in Man,** and **We Are Future.**

ROGER TROISFONTAINES, S.J. has degrees in letters, classical philology, philosophy and theology from the University of Louvain. He is director of studies and professor at the Jesuit Faculties of Namur, Belgium. He has lectured widely in France, Belgium, England and the U.S.A. He is author of several books, among them **Existentialism and Christian Thought** and **I Do Not Die.**

JÜRGEN MOLTMANN is professor of systematic theology in the Evangelical Faculty of Theology at the University of Tübingen, Germany. He was visiting professor at Duke University from September, 1967 to April, 1968. He has traveled and lectured widely in the academic centers of America and Europe. His recent publications include **The Theology of Hope, Religion, Revolution and the Future,** and **Hope and Planning.**

KILIAN McDONNELL, O.S.B. is professor in the graduate school of St. John's University, Collegeville, Minnesota and executive director of its Institute for Ecumenical and Cultural Research. He has served as scripture editor for **Worship** and editor of **Sponsa Regis.** Contributor of numerous articles to theological journals, he is the author of **John Calvin, the Church and the Eucharist.**

MICHAEL J. TAYLOR, S.J. holds an S.T.D. degree from Woodstock College and is presently professor of theology at Seattle University. He has written and lectured widely on ecumenical and sacramental topics. Because of his contributions to the field of ecumenics he has been awarded a Lilly Post-Doctoral Fellowship in Religion. Among his published works are **Liturgy and Christian Unity, The Sacred and the Secular, The Mystery of Sin and Forgiveness,** and **Sex: Thoughts for Contemporary Christians.**